Melanie Bishop
630 Morrell Blvd.
Prescott, AZ   86301

A
Little
more
about
me

ALSO BY PAM HOUSTON

Waltzing the Cat

Cowboys Are My Weakness

Women on Hunting: Essays, Fiction, and Poetry (Ed.)

For Melanie

A
Little
More
about
Me

With gratitude
Take Car
Pam Houston

W. W. NORTON & COMPANY · NEW YORK LONDON

Line from Poem VII of "Twenty-One Love Poems" and lines from
"Origins and History of Consciousness," from *The Dream of a Common
Language: Poems 1974–1977* by Adrienne Rich. Copyright © 1978 by
W. W. Norton & Company, Inc. Reprinted by permission of the author
and W. W. Norton & Company, Inc. Lines from Part I, "A dark woman,
head bent, listening for something," from "An Atlas of the Difficult
World," from *An Atlas of the Difficult World: Poems 1998–1991* by
Adrienne Rich. Copyright © 1991 by Adrienne Rich. Reprinted
by permission of the author and W. W. Norton & Company, Inc.

For information about permission to reproduce selections from this
book, write to Permissions, W. W. Norton & Company, Inc., 500 Fifth
Avenue, New York, NY 10110

The text of this book is composed in Granjon
with the display set in Democratica
Desktop composition by Gina Webster
Manufacturing by Quebecor Printing, Fairfield, Inc.

Library of Congress Cataloging-in-Publication Data
Houston, Pam.
A little more about me / Pam Houston.
p.   cm.
ISBN 0-393-04805-5
1. Houston, Pam. 2. Women authors, American—20th
century—biography. 3. Voyages and travels. I. Title.
PS3558.08725Z468   1999
814'.54—dc21   99-25336
CIP

W. W. Norton & Company, Inc., 500 Fifth Avenue, New York, N.Y. 10110
www.wwnorton.com

W. W. Norton & Company Ltd., 10 Coptic Street, London WC1A 1PU

1 2 3 4 5 6 7 8 9 0

Acknowledgments

Some of the essays in this collection appeared, sometimes in slightly different form, in the following publications: *Allure*: "The Morality of Fat"; *Condé Nast Sports for Women*: "A Man Who'll Freeze His Eyelashes for You" and "Pregnancy and Other Natural Disasters"; *Elle*: "In the Company of Fishermen" and "Redefining Success"; *Mirabella*: "African Nights"; the *New York Times*: "A River Runs Through Them"; *Outside*: "Powerhouse by the Book"; *Park City Magazine*: "The Bad Dogs of Park City" and "The Pit Bull and the Mountain Goat"; *Ski*: "On (Not) Climbing the Grand Teton" and "Growing Apart: Leaving Park City," which has been combined with "The Pit Bull and the Mountain Goat" in this volume; *Travel & Leisure*: "Waves Every Color of Harvest" and "Soul of the Andes"; *Vogue*: "Eight Days in the Brooks Range with April and the Boys"; *Whitefish Magazine*: "Looking for Abbey's Lion."

"Out of Habit, I Start Apologizing" first appeared in the anthology *Minding the Body*; and "The Blood of Fine and Wild Animals" first appeared in the anthology *Women on Hunting*. "In the Company of Fishermen" was anthologized in *A Different*

Angle and *Gifts of the Wild*; "Eight Days in the Brooks Range with April and the Boys" was anthologized in *The Writing Path 2*; "A River Runs Through Them" was anthologized in *Walking the Twilight 2*; and "On (Not) Climbing the Grand Teton" was anthologized in *Wild Places*.

I am grateful to all the editors who helped bring these essays to their present form, especially Karen Marta for her irreverence and Pat Towers for hearing the rhythm of my sentences and making me smarter than I am. I thank Kerry Tessaro for her last-minute expertise. As always, I am grateful to Carol Houck Smith. No one on earth loves books more.

This book is for
Marilyn Shannahan
Sarah Phipps
and
Betsy Marino

And in memory of
Sally Quinters

Eventually I realized that wanting to go where I hadn't been might be as fruitful as going there; but for the repose of my soul I had to do both.

—Seamus O'Banion

And I wake up, and I ask myself what state I'm in,
And I say well I'm lucky cause I am like East Berlin,
I had this wall, and what I knew of the free world
Was that I could see their fireworks and I could hear their radio. . . .

—Dar Williams

Contents

A few good men

one long look in the mirror

Dispatches from five continents

Home is where your Dogs are

The
Long way
to safety

The Long Way
to Safety

Early this summer, I paid $4,500 for a horse. He's beautiful: a quarter-horse gelding nearly seventeen hands high, the grandson of the nationally famous Two-Eyed Jack, a blue roan with rust-colored markings on his face who in the sunlight looks like he's sculpted out of Oreo cookie ice cream. His name is Roany, evidence of a slight lack of imagination on the part of the cowboy named Skip who sold him to me. Skip is good at being a cowboy though, and if Roany's anything to go on, even better at training a horse.

I've been driving to New Mexico to ride Roany once a week for the last couple of months, testing him in every circumstance that I can think of to see how he responds to trouble on the trail. We've crossed rivers, negotiated highways, hurried across slippery blacktop parking lots, and chased off a whole pack of snarling Doberman-mix dogs. We've ridden through culverts under interstate highways where I had less than two inches clearance between my head and the structural concrete above me, and we've sidled up to barbed-wire gates so I could lean over and open them without getting off.

In eight four-hour rides the only time I felt Roany's body tense was when an Air Force bomber executed an alarmingly low flyby in the middle of a spring thunderstorm, and even then he got over his minor panic before I had time to get scared. The words I keep using to describe Roany to my friends are *centered* and *balanced*. Being on his back, being in his presence, is a little like being in the presence of a Zen master. It's not just that he doesn't make me nervous, it's that he makes me calm beyond my wildest dreams. Skip says it even more simply: he calls Roany the horse with the heart of gold.

I have always owned psychotic horses. Savannah, my Morgan mare, had a thing about scraping me off on tree branches and flying into bucking frenzies whenever she got bored. Willy, a thoroughbred quarter-horse mix, had been drugged to make him faster on the track when he was younger. He seemed perfectly calm until one day he had a flashback and shattered my forearm so badly the doctors had to remove nineteen pieces of bone. Deseo, who is a perfect gentleman around the barn and a star in any ring or arena, works himself up into such a fear frenzy whenever we go out on the trail that there is often nothing for me to do but get off him, try to calm him, and lead him quietly back to the barn.

There are no problem horses, say the equine gurus of the day, and I am 100 percent sure the fault in all of these cases is mine. When I bought each of these horses they were young, untrained, and inexpensive (except Savannah, who was free; I should have known she might have some problems when her owner said he'd pay me to get her out of his sight for good). And hard as I might try, however much book and clinic knowledge I can put behind me, I am simply not connected securely enough to myself to train young horses properly. I believe I'm getting closer, but I'm not there yet.

For the last twenty years, I had everyone convinced I wasn't afraid of anything; but try telling that story to a horse when you are sitting on his back. Horses know the truth about how you are feeling faster than you have time to think it, no matter how hard you try to appear confident and calm. Horses are perfect mirrors of the psyche, seeing through manipulation and deceit and then acting out whatever fear picture you've shown them.

This may be why, in spite of a handful of fairly serious injuries, I have never stopped riding horses. Even in my most locked-up periods of denial, I wanted to be in the presence of somebody or something who knew the deepest truth about me.

I started riding when I was eight years old, at about the same time I stopped crying when things hurt me and just before I stopped admitting I was ever scared. I spent every afternoon and most weekends at one barn or another, cleaning stalls in exchange for lessons and trail rides. I went to the barn because it was a good way to escape my parents' house, which in those years was full of disappointment and anger.

Even then, I felt understood by the horses. When we communicated well, and they timed the jump over the hedgerow perfectly, or sidestepped a neat diagonal across the dressage ring, I felt like I'd been given a gift by a friend. And when they wouldn't listen to me, when they refused a jump and I went tumbling headfirst into the wooden standards, when they fell out of a fast canter and into an extended trot, and the teacher yelled at me in her German accent, "He can tell you are afraid, he can tell you don't really want to do it!" I would be half chagrined and half delighted. I really *didn't* want to do the scary thing—ever. The horse, in all his equine wisdom, was in perfect agreement with me.

Then I grew up and got so far away from myself that the word *afraid* ceased to be part of my vocabulary. By my sixteenth birthday I had walked away from sixteen serious automobile accidents. In more than half of them, the car I was in was totaled; in more than half of them, a great deal of alcohol was involved. My mother drove a Plymouth Fury right through a 7-Eleven, my father rolled a Cadillac Seville nine times on Christmas Eve, my best high school girlfriend put us and her Ford station wagon under a semi, right at decapitation level.

My reasoning must have been along the lines of *If I'm not dead yet, I must have drawn a real lucky number.*

I entered adulthood seeking out one life-threatening adventure after another, and the ones that I didn't seek out seemed determined to find me. Hurricanes, tornadoes, avalanches, and hundred-year floods followed me around the globe like a pack of unruly dogs, and I never seemed to have access to shelter when they caught up. I bought horses that would stand as monuments to my bravery, and I got hurt, and I got hurt again, and I followed the old cowboy rule and always got back on. In time the thing I valued most about myself was my level-headed courage in the face of (usually self-inflicted) danger. In time it became the thing other people valued most about me.

Therapists have told me that I am determined to recreate the danger I faced daily in my childhood, putting myself at risk again and again, as if it would give me some retroactive feeling of control. Their hypothesis might explain several of my less successful relationships. It definitely explains the psychotic horses. It probably also explains the avalanches and hundred-year floods. But I don't want it to explain why I love a good adventure. I don't want it to explain why I love to be outdoors.

Happy-to-be-alive adrenaline is a powerful and addicting substance, and I've had a lifetime's worth of it, in less than half a lifetime's years. But I can't deny the unadulterated joy I have felt in each adventure, a joy so pure it must be separate from the addiction. Sitting safe on the other side of those high-risk years, there isn't one heart-stopping moment I would have wanted to miss out on, not one where the life experience gains—in retrospect—didn't exceed the terror and discomfort level at the time.

Our mid-thirties is the time when most of us stop bouncing and start breaking. It's an age when we begin to fear that our luck may run out. I've been trying, these last few years, to find a way to hold on to the joy of adventuring while I also try to shed my penchant for unnecessary risk.

The Buddhists believe that before they begin the life-changing work of their Zen practice, the world is exactly how it appears. *Mountains are mountains*, they are famous for saying, *and rivers are rivers*.

Once they start to meditate, though, to lose themselves in the change that must occur, mountains cease to be mountains and rivers cease to be rivers. The Zen student loses the points of reference he has always relied upon: mountains overlap and dissolve into rivers, rivers break their barriers and rise up like mountains, and the student becomes less and less sure about who and what he is, dissolving his sense of self within a dissolving world.

With enough understanding and practice, things click back into place: mountains go back to being mountains and rivers go back to being rivers. But meditation has moved the student to a place where he can see that the mountains exist in relationship to the rivers and that they make each other possible. He has opened his eyes to the interrelatedness of everything, including the world and himself.

In the last few years, all my mountains became rivers and all my rivers became mountains. In the most literal sense, I found myself negotiating rivers when they fell down rapids as steep as the sides of mountains, and I learned that rather than climbing to the top of mountains, I preferred to walk around them, to encircle them, the way a river would. I also lost every reference point that had kept me grounded in my fearless and emotionless life. The next thing I knew all the big words had started to shift on me: Adventure, Success, Friendship, Marriage, Feminism, Love, Morality, Home, Safety—before long I wasn't able to make anything stand still. Everything that was a mountain in me turned into a river. I don't know how long it will take until I'm part mountain again.

When I was in graduate school, my professors told me that there was no reality outside of language, that the desk where I was sitting, frantically scribbling notes, didn't exist unless I called it a desk, and for quite a while I believed them.

I didn't understand then that theirs was a belief system that, among other things, let us all off the hook. If there were no desks, then certainly there were no polluted rivers; if there were no chairs there was no poverty; if there were no walls and windows, there was no pain or violence in our homes. If the world could only be talked—or written—into being, we would only have to take responsibility for what we said, and never what we did.

Perhaps I took what my professors said too literally, but I finally left graduate school five years into it, only six months before I could have walked away with my Ph.D.

It was a typical day in the English department, and I had been waiting in the office to get a piece of paper signed that said I was teaching a class that didn't exist, so that imaginary money could be transferred from one department to another, to pay my tuition for the class that another piece of paper said I was taking, which didn't exist either. Two of my professors walked in and had a twenty-minute conversation over the Xerox machine about the relative merits of *imminence* and *eminence*.

Never mind that I knew that both of these men were facing tragedies of the highest order in their lives. Never mind that our country was about to go to war again for reasons that none of us understood. Never mind that sixteen inches of snow had fallen on the peaks just outside the window and was making the world look like the paradise it might have been if only we could see it.

For the first time since I had become a graduate student, it occurred to me to be astonished at all the things my professors weren't saying to each other. For the first time it occurred to me that my professors might be wrong. There *was* a world that existed outside of language, and I had been away from it far too long. I left the office that day without getting my paper signed, and I never went back.

I understand now, but only *just* now, that my premature departure from the university may have been not a failure, but a success, the very first time I acted on a belief that was entirely mine and entirely unpopular. I loved the university, and had I stayed I probably would have done everything in my power to make it love me back, to become one of those professors I still greatly admire, to be imminently on the verge of eminence, to live in a world where there really are only words.

I also understand now that it was not such a bad thing for a young writer to believe that the world is made of language in the same way it might be good for a sculptor to believe that the world is made of clay. I learned language games in grad school that I still haven't tired of playing, and it was those professors who taught me how to make the words dance.

What I know for certain is that when I left graduate school I reentered the world with a hunger for it that I had never felt before. I felt nothing short of ecstasy seeing a cottonwood tree, a clearwater stream, a Bhutanese child, or a sled dog in harness and realizing—like waking up safe in my bedroom after a dream that my house burned down—that the world is real, all of it, and it had been waiting for me all that time to wake up and begin my day.

The essays in this book are a result of that continuing reentry. You will find them full of all the real things: rain forests and deserts and osprey and oceans, mountain goats and river ice and camping trips and wine. You will find grizzly bears and gynecologists, silver mines and steelhead fishermen, human stoplights and junkyard horses, a few good men, and a lot of good dogs. You will find the Tetons, the Wasatch, the

Andes, the Himalayas, the Brooks Range, and the San Juan, the Main Salmon, the Dolores, the Colorado, and the Rhone, the Kalahari, the Great Basin, the North Slope, and the Pacific Rim. There is a hippopotamus named Esmerelda, a wolfhound named Dante, and a Buddhist named Karma, proving again what we've always suspected: that fiction has nothing at all on real life.

The essays in this book have been written over a period of five years. In that time I have run more than forty whitewater rivers. I have hiked in the backcountry more than three thousand miles. I have visited forty-three countries on five continents. I have had search parties sent out for me twice. I have been on more than four hundred planes. I have been told to get into crash position for landing four times. I have gotten immunizations for every disease the world has to offer. I have been mugged three times, always in the San Francisco Bay Area. I have been to every United State except North Dakota. I have put a total of four hundred thousand miles on three different cars.

In addition to the travel that has set the pace and the rhythm of my life, several things happened to me during these years that I wouldn't have expected. I was married to and left a man I thought I would be with forever. I made a best friend and then watched her slowly die. I had a dog I thought irreplaceable, and then I replaced him with one I may love even more. I lost my mother to heart failure, and in a more metaphorical sense, I lost my father that way too. In the process I regained a childhood I had almost forgotten. I made some new friends, and lost even more than I made. (*You need six in the end to carry your coffin*, is what my friend Jack Hicks says.) I bought a house that came with a great big mortgage, a truck with automatic doors and windows, a dog with a family tree much taller than mine.

I moved twice in the last five years, from Park City, Utah, to Oakland, California, and then back to the Rocky Mountains, to a town called Creede, Colorado, which I believe with all my heart will be my permanent home.

The road I've taken these five years has been a long and twisted one. A weathered sign stuck into the dirt by the side of it reads *The Long Way to Safety*, and I can see by the grass growing up along the yellow line down the middle that this isn't the route Triple A recommends.

Through the windshield I can see everything I want to take with me: horses and men and mountains and rivers. But in the rearview mirror, damned if I don't see horses and men and mountains and rivers, everything I need to leave behind. On both sides of the car, horses and men and mountains and rivers, and I'm just trying to keep it between the lines. Two wheels off one side and I know I'll lose something essential, two wheels off the other and I'll wind up paralyzed or dead.

Only in the throes of a life-and-death situation, my therapists used to say, *will you feel comfortable and safe*, and I'm dedicated these days to proving them wrong. I've stopped running rivers at high water, and I've sworn off even *trying* to climb the kind of mountain that requires hardware and a rope. In situations that are harder to call, I question my intentions and try to stay one step ahead of the danger. If I crawl several hundred yards into a crumbling silver mine in Bolivia, I want it to be because I will learn something about the miners' humanity. If I have a heart attack at seventeen thousand feet in Bhutan, I want to have something in my first-aid kit that will help.

There are people—a lot of them—who have resisted my desire to change, who believe it is more important than ever for women to prove they are Amazonian. When I read my essay "On (Not) Climbing the Grand Teton" to a group of outdoorswomen in Wyoming they all leapt to make excuses for me, low biorhythms or PMS, and they finally wound up blaming it on my guide.

I tried to explain to them that for me, in this case, true success lay within the failure, in listening to my fear and standing firm in my desire to go back down the mountain, but they wouldn't hear of it. That same month I was told by an editor who wanted me to go sky *surfing* (*sky surfing!?*) that I'd have a hard time getting assignments if I wasn't willing to stay out there *on the edge*. But how many times can you walk to the same edge and find it interesting? And now that I've begun to step back off the one that was my nemesis, I see new, more interesting edges everywhere I look: artistic, spiritual, emotional, even physical edges that don't necessarily involve risking my life.

I finally sold my Morgan mare, Savannah, because everyone I knew said she was going to kill me. I sold Willy because the doctor told me it would take more than two years to repair my arm. I still have high hopes for Deseo—evidence not of success, but neither of failure. If Roany has the same effect on him that he has on me, everything ought to work out just fine.

So now Roany's out there in the pasture, pulling up the first of the spring grasses and looking like cookies and cream. Tomorrow, for the first time since he's been mine, I'm going to throw a saddle on him and ride up into the mountains. I'm starting to suspect that the old saying about getting right back on the horse that's thrown you may be overrated. I'm learning to say *I don't know* when I don't and *Yes* when I do and *That hurts* or *I like you* right as it's happening. I'm wondering how much longer my mountains will need to be rivers. I'm finally wrenching my mind around to the fact that Roany is worth $4,500 *because* he is safe and gentle. In my life, more to the point, he's priceless.

DOGS
and other
REASONS
to Live

The Bad Dogs
of Park City

L egend has it that in the old days packs of wild pigs used to roam the streets of Park City, and that's how the leniency toward wandering dogs began. Whether it's true or not, it's a great story, one that makes us think that the occasional group of bad dogs we see headed down Main Street, as if on assignment, are part of our history, something we all should be proud of, something we should leave well enough alone.

But Park City is quickly becoming a town full of civilized people, and civilized people, I'm told, don't let their dogs run loose. The animal control officers say that loose dogs will be impounded, and repeat offenders will be put down. Park City Friends of the Animals says that anyone who can't keep their dogs at home shouldn't own a dog. And there is a certain logic to that. But those of us who own dogs who are smarter than we are, dogs who consider themselves part of this town's local color, dogs who manage to come and go under their own free will with help, it seems, only from other dogs, dogs who are often in trouble with the dogcatcher, dogs who in some cases have a price on their heads—those of us who own the dogs of Park City whom, try as we might, we cannot keep at home—we might argue that our dogs help make the town what it is.

My dog's name is Jackson. He's long and lean and blond and big-nosed. He rides around town in the back of his red pickup, which he occasionally lets me drive, and he has the dubious distinction of having the loudest bark of any dog in Park City (possibly in the intermountain west). He is as cool as a bad dog can be. He's a little embarrassed about me, because I'm not really very cool at all, but I try to make it up to him by letting him go to all the best parties. He has way more friends in this town than I do, human and canine, and a few more enemies. He's been arrested twice, once for begging hamburgers at the Corner Store, and subsequently trying to follow his benefactors into the gondola, and once in Salt Lake City for threatening to bite a young Mormon boy, who Jackson swears to me was trying to steal the truck (the little boy was eight). Jackson has come out of the back of the pickup three times, all at speeds over sixty miles an hour; two of those times he suffered nothing more than a road rash, and the third time was in Heber City, and I swear he did it just to see if he could beat me home. (And he did.) Jackson likes to hang out with Roger's mastiff Bo and P.J.'s husky Raichle; he tolerates Hailey, my other dog, who is decidedly uncool; but his favorite dumpstering buddy will always be Rasta.

I like to think of Rasta as the patriarch of all the dogs on Main Street. Rasta was introduced to me as the baddest dog in Park City, and though he's never so much as nipped at an irritating human, he has a reputation for being able to kick any dog's butt. He's also earned respect among the local canines for the most creative dumpstering techniques of any dog. Two visitors once reported to his mom, Christie, that they saw him line a dog called Arlo up in front of Cisero's dumpster, and then use Arlo's back as a springboard to get inside. Rasta claims he's learned everything he knows from Helmet, Sonny's late rugby dog, the only dog that Rasta ever let push him around. But Rasta's life hasn't been all glory and garbage. He's done some hard time in the slammer; he saw his very best dog-friend Bakkhus gunned down outside Kamas for allegedly chasing deer, on a day he got shot at himself but managed to run between the bullets. Rasta lives the quiet life in Kamas now, but he and Christie come to Park City every day. You can see him in front of her office on lower Main Street, too old and wise, now, to get into much trouble, but still proud and friendly, as much a part of Main Street as the sidewalk on which he sits.

When I tried to find Fred, the chocolate Lab that has hung out in front of the Alamo for as long as I can remember, the response among his human friends was universal. "Oh, shit," they said. "Is he in trouble again?"

But when I finally caught up with Fred, at his new hangout in the back room of the snowboard shop where his owner, Mikk, works, he tried to play down his criminal record. Instead, he wanted to talk about his six-year residency that he feels gives him status as a local. "A lot of dogs come and go," Fred said, stretching his long chocolate body between a workbench on the left and a row of new snowboards on the right, "but I was born here." Fred prides himself on being a totally self-sufficient dog. He says he used to go dumpstering when he was young, and it was what all the dogs were doing, but now he finds it's quicker and easier to stand in front of the Claim Jumper, put his sad dog face on, and bark occasionally until someone comes out and gives him a rib bone. Mikk tells me that once a bunch of guys at the Alamo put a sign around Fred's neck that said WILL WORK FOR FOOD. "It was good grub that night," Fred admits, "but I do fine without the sign."

Tyler is one of the few dogs in Park City who actually works for a living. Since 1985 Tyler has been the official Park City Ski Patrol Search and Rescue Dog, and if you spend any time in Jupiter Bowl, you've seen him riding the chair lift, sometimes with Kenny Elliott, his handler, sometimes all by himself. Maybe you've seen him on the snowmobile with Kenny, paws up on the handlebars, big doggie grin on his face, but a snowmobile is pup's play to a dog who has been, many times, in a helicopter, and who has even been air-evacuated out of the gondola. Tyler works on the mountain one hundred days a year, mostly practicing for the live rescues he and Kenny both hope will never come. "Tyler does all the work," Kenny says. "I learned most of what I know about snow rescues by watching his signs and clues." Tyler has never been picked up by the dogcatcher, a message to all the other Park City dogs about clean living and hard work. Like many of the Park City powder hounds, Tyler spends his summers windsurfing, with Kenny, in the Columbia River gorge.

The only physical difference between Tyler and his son Astro is that Tyler's left ear flops and Astro's right ear flops. The metaphysical differences between the dogs are many. Whether the flopping ears indicate something about the working capacities of the dogs' left and right brains would be an interesting question for dog psychologists, but for each day

Tyler has spent hard at work on the mountain, Astro has spent another day begging burgers and running from the law. Astro doesn't look like a delinquent: he's big and sweet and he likes, about as much as anything, to simply chase rocks. What he also likes to chase, unfortunately for him and John, his owner, is the bull wheel on the bottom of the Pay Day chairlift, and he barks at it until he drives the lifties so crazy they have to call the pound. Astro's been picked up so many times now that the last time he got busted they took him and John away in cuffs with a thousand-dollar bail on John, a seven-hundred-dollar bond on Astro, and a promise to have the dog put to sleep if he ever got picked up again. "Astro's been clean now for a year," John says proudly, while Astro barks happily at a rock between his feet. "Kenny says I've ruined him, that I should have sent him to some Swiss school of avalanche and doggie etiquette, but he's the best construction dog in the world, and that's the way I like him."

A relatively new addition to the Park City dog scene is Bo, an English mastiff who is quickly becoming the most pho-tographed tourist attraction in Park City. Only three years old and weighing in at over 150 pounds, Bo has charmed his way into the heart of every visitor who lays eyes on him; he winds up in their photo albums, their video libraries, and even a few of their condos and cars. "Bo finds himself in some strange places," Roger tells me from behind the bar at the Alamo, "but I always get a call. People love him until they find out how much they'd have to feed him, then they let him out and he finds his way home." Roger is too Park City–cool to admit that Bo's celebrity status pleases him, but when he tells me Bo has been on David Letterman, a grin crosses his face that speaks nothing but fatherly pride. "Some celebrity was visiting Park City and took his photo, and he held it up on the show," Roger says, the grin getting even bigger as he hands the waitress a couple of beers. "I don't want it going to his head, though," he says. As anyone can see, Bo's head is already big enough.

There's no way to write about all the famous and infamous dogs of Park City. Already I see that I'm leaving out Lee's little mutt Arrow, rescued by Lee from former owners who used to feed him hallucinogenic mushrooms and then tie him up. I'm leaving out Stephanie and Dana's dog Pan, named for his ability to disappear, and Marty, who lived for years on the roof of the Alamo. I'm leaving out Max, the young dalmatian, and the doggie surprise party Mitchie had for him when he turned three. Then there's Jersey Dave's dog Arlo; Yuki, the biggest dog in town, on Upper Norfolk; Chaos and Bigsey on Prospect; and Cody, whom the Austrians seem to have adopted, on lower King Road.

To say that the dogs of Park City are intelligent, to say that they can communicate with each other, is to grossly understate the obvious. To say they have the most organized social structure since Lenin and Marx is a little more to the point. If there is any doubt about whether or not these dogs can systematically work together, ask Stephanie and Dana how Bo and his husky sidekicks come and get Pan off his chain without any human assistance; watch Rasta organize a dumpster raid as smoothly and efficiently as a union boss. If you don't believe these dogs are as capable as any human being of independent and original thought, watch Bo sweet-talk a visitor out of what she thought was tomorrow's lunch, watch Fred stand up casually and stretch and move toward the door every night at five minutes to ten, just as dishwashers all over town carry that night's leftovers to the dumpsters that wait in Swede Alley.

We humans moved to Park City, many of us, because it offered us the chance to be our truest selves, to lead an independent lifestyle, to not be tied (or chained) to the conventions of a confining city life. Should we expect our dogs to want anything less? More and more, these days, I let my dogs show me how to be happy, how to make choices, how to live my life, and I'm not the only one. You've seen the way dog stars are splashed across the hot new books and movies; you know dog therapy is being used as a doctor-prescribed treatment in hospitals. How many children do you think Pan has greeted on Main Street? How many guests have had the pleasure of giving Jackson a pet and a slice of pizza at the Pizza Co.? How many smiles has Astro brought vacationing tourists as he chases the bull wheel round and round? Speaking for myself, I know there's very little wrong with me that the sight of Bo loping up Main Street can't cure, and when I see a couple of dogs making tracks down Main Street with something I can only guess at on their minds, it makes me feel good that I live in a town where occasionally dogs can get free and occasionally their owners can let them.

I was in the post office, checking my mail, when a young man came in with a black Lab puppy, no bigger than the top of one of his Sorels. The puppy was adorable, floppy-eared, with feet way too big for the rest of him, and he ran circles around his owner's feet, bumping softly into an occasional bystander. One woman, actually a little doglike herself,

dressed in black pants, black turtleneck, black jacket, black hair
hanging over her face, hissed, "They don't belong in here." The
young man was apologetic; he picked his puppy up and took
him outside. I left the post office incredibly depressed, because
while I couldn't in good faith argue that yes, dogs do belong in
the post office, I also couldn't allow myself to face the fact that
this is what we are becoming, a town where a ski bum with a
puppy is a criminal and the post office is a place we go to make
each other feel bad.

One day, years ago, when I was complaining about how
hard it was to find a place to live that allowed dogs, a friend of
mine said, with considerable wisdom, that having dogs forces
us to keep living in places that are right for us. And I think of
all the things I might have given up had my dogs not shown
me what was important in my life: fresh air, a garden, an
eleven-thousand-foot mountain in my backyard. And whether
or not the pig story is true, I think we should accept the fact
that a doggie culture seems to be a part of every ski town in
America: Winter Park, Steamboat, Sun Valley—the dogs are
one of the ways we show the visitors we are free.

I was in Telluride in February, and I had the pleasure of
meeting Zudnick, Tyler's more famous counterpart at that
resort, who unlike Tyler has a history with the dogcatcher a
mile wide. Zudnick had his one last chance and lost it, and
was on doggie death row, no appeal pending. But the towns-
people of Telluride loved Zudnick, and so did all the children
at the county hospital, where he worked as a volunteer. The
children wrote letters and the town drew up a petition, and
Zudnick was saved from the gas chamber to ride the chairlifts
again.

I met a man in Manhattan last winter who had lived in Park City during the mid-seventies. "You wouldn't have believed it," he told me. "Park City was full of dogs then. There were leash laws, of course, but somehow the dogs got around them. The dogcatcher was always busy, and still you couldn't walk down Main Street at any time of day without seeing a dog or two." The man didn't understand, right away, why I broke out laughing. He didn't understand how happy I was to know that in this town that is changing at such a dizzying rate a few things remain the same. He didn't understand how his words gave me hope that in five or ten or twenty years Park City will still be a place where we can find bad dogs, free and happy, with big things on their minds, walking past us on the street.

Looking for
Abbey's Lion

When I was a senior in college in Ohio, when the farthest west I had been was across the Indiana border one drunken night when a boyfriend and I drove in to my mother's hometown and stole the Lions Club's *Welcome to Spiceland, Indiana* sign, a good friend introduced me to the works of Edward Abbey. I devoured *Desert Solitaire* first, then *The Journey Home*, *Down the River*, *Beyond the Wall*, *Black Sun*, and *The Monkey Wrench Gang*. Abbey lived in the heart of wild country I could scarcely imagine as I looked out over those low green midwestern hills. Jagged granite peaks, silver in the twilight, bright orange labyrinths of twisted sandstone, wide rivers of thick muddy water moving through canyon walls five times higher than the tallest hill I could see from my dorm. The fact that Abbey was, like me, from a small town in Pennsylvania seemed rife with significance. If he could claim the west as his latter-day home, perhaps one day I could too.

Of all Abbey's writing that stays in my accessible memory, my favorite passage is one that appears in *The Journey Home* in an essay titled "Freedom and Wilderness, Wilderness and Freedom." Abbey is doing his usual canyon hike: too long, no water, too close to dark. He's found some mountain lion tracks halfway up the canyon, and since he's never seen a mountain lion, he's decided to follow them. But night comes down on him quickly, and he's forced to give up the search and turn around. As he walks through the gathering darkness toward the mouth of the canyon he hears footsteps behind him, once, twice, three times. They seem to stop when he stops, begin again when he walks on. Fear mounting inside of him, he swivels, suddenly, sharp and fast, and sees the lion, only fifty yards behind him, massive in the twilight and sleek, one paw raised in the air as if in greeting, yellow eyes, unblinking and cool. Abbey holds out his own hand, and takes three slow steps toward the cat before he comes to his senses and decides he's not quite ready to shake a mountain lion's paw. The lion watches Abbey descend toward what's left of the light at the bottom of the canyon, unmoving, paw still raised.

The magic of that passage for me is contained in the moment of decision, the tension between Abbey's wanting to embrace that lion as if they were friends who'd met up after many years' separation, and his eventual respect for the lion's wildness, his recognition of the distance that must be maintained between the wild thing and himself, his understanding that wanting to shake the lion's paw must, for the time being, be enough.

I read that essay eleven years ago not knowing, in any exact sense, what a mountain lion looked like, not knowing, for that matter, what a canyon hike was. The one thing I did know, even then, is that I wanted to feel the spark of raw, communicable energy that translated between man and beast in Abbey's story, and that if I could ever stand face to face for even one brief moment with a mountain lion I would learn something invaluable about my life.

I headed west for the first time at the end of my senior year, and from the Missouri border on I kept my eyes trained on the sagebrush-sided highways, on the dense rocky outcroppings, hoping for a glimpse of Abbey's lion. And that first, awe-filled summer, when it seemed I couldn't keep my eyes open wide enough, long enough, to take the big country in, when it seemed I couldn't listen hard enough, breathe fast enough, walk far enough to do the land any kind of justice, I added hike after hike to my new life's list of accomplishments, my eyes always ready for a flash of feline muscle, my ears straining for the soft fall of padded feet. I sighted fresh tracks once, and older ones maybe half a dozen times, but I never rounded the corner in time to see the tip of a tail disappearing, and no yellow eyes ever turned around to follow me back down canyon, no muscley beast ever raised his paw in salute to me.

The west captured my soul and imagination like nothing before in my life. I cut my ties to the east and moved west permanently, my jobs cycling through the seasons, changing always in the direction of less and less pay per hour, and more and more hours outside. From a bartender to a bus driver to a highway flagger to a park ranger paid only as a volunteer, I finally settled into a career as a river and wilderness guide, my hours outside outnumbering those inside by almost four to one.

In eleven years of hiking, boating, guiding, and exploring I've come face to face with nearly every North American game species. I've watched a female black bear and her cubs gorge themselves on huckleberries, heard a big bull elk bugling not ten feet from my ear. I've had a timber wolf walk right through my campsite as if he intended to join me for dinner, and I've had an abandoned mule deer fawn come and eat grass out of my hand. I've walked through thick pine trees right into the knees of a confused cow moose, opened my eyes in the middle of the night to the inquisitive sniffing of a porcupine, watched a group of bighorn lambs play a very complicated game of King of the Hill on a craggy peak not twenty yards away. I've seen the hot puffy breath of a bison break the clarity of a frozen Yellowstone morning, and the first white fur of winter appear on the considerable feet of a snowshoe hare. I've followed a single coyote for miles across slickrock in hazy moonlight, and walked among a herd of pronghorn in the still heat of a high desert day. I've watched lynx, bobcat, ptarmigan, rattlesnake, golden eagles, whitetails, javelinas, hawks, and stumbled across more big male grizzly bears than any one person ought to be allowed and still be around to tell about it. But I've still never come face to face with Abbey's lion.

It is clear to me, only now, that I came to live in the west not because I would see a mountain lion, but because I might see one. (If what I really wanted was to see a mountain lion I could have lived down the street from the Bronx Zoo.) And though I couldn't have imagined it from my dorm room in Ohio, the mountain lion has taught me his lesson not through a face-to-face encounter but through his elusiveness and intangibility. The mountain lion's lesson for me has been one of patience; even more correctly, it has been a lesson in the value of uncaptured dreams. For much as I have loved the heart-stopping surprise of my encounters with bear, with wolf, with coyote, they cannot match the power and purity of my unrequited desire to see Abbey's lion. A dream unrealized, the lion has taught me, is the essential food of the soul.

And I have imagined him, so many times, the way he will stand, his fur, shades of dusky gold in the late-afternoon sunlight, his eyes suggesting a game I'll most likely not play. He is with me always, this lion of my imagination. He will keep my eyes wide open as I'm walking through the canyons. He will keep my love of and wonder at the landscape that surrounds me ever rare, ever young.

The Blood of Fine
and Wild Animals

When I was twenty-six years old, I fell in love with a man who was a hunting guide. We didn't have what you would call the healthiest of relationships. He was selfish, evasive, and unfaithful. I was demanding, manipulative, and self-pitying. He was a Republican and I was a Democrat. He was a Texan and I was not. I belonged to the Sierra Club and he belonged to the NRA. Yet somehow we managed to stay together for three years of our lives, and to spend two solid months of each of those three years hunting for Dall sheep in Alaska.

I was always quick, in those days, to make the distinction between a hunter and a hunting guide, for though I was indirectly responsible for the deaths of a total of five animals, I have never killed an animal myself, and never intend to. I had the opportunity once to shoot a Dall ram whose horns were so big it would have likely gotten my name into the record books. I had three decent men applying every kind of peer pressure they could come up with, and I even went so far as to raise the rifle to my eye, unsure in that moment what I would do next. But once I got it up there I couldn't think of one good reason to pull the trigger.

I learned about bullets and guns and caliber and spotting scopes, and I was a good hunting guide simply because I'm good at the outdoors. I can carry a heavy pack long distances. I can cook great meals on a backpacking stove. I keep my humor pretty well for weeks without a toilet or a shower. I can sleep, if I have to, on a forty-five-degree ledge of ice. I know how to move in the wilderness, and because of this I understand how the sheep move. I'm a decent tracker. I've got what they call *animal sense*.

When I was hunting Dall sheep in Alaska it was one on one on one. One hunter, one guide, one ram that we tracked, normally for ten days, before we got close enough to shoot it. My obvious responsibility was to the hunter. It was my job to keep him from falling into a crevasse or getting eaten by a grizzly bear, to carry his gun when he got too tired, to keep him fed and watered, to listen to his stories, to get him up at three in the morning and keep him on his feet till midnight, to drag him fifteen miles and sometimes as much as four thousand vertical feet a day, and if everything went well, to get him in position to shoot a sheep to take home and put on his wall. My other job, though understated, was to protect the sheep from the hunters, to guarantee that the hunter shot only the oldest ram in the herd, that he only shot at one animal, and that he only fired when he was close enough to make a killing shot. A hunter can't walk a wounded animal down across the glaciers in Alaska the way he can through the trees in the Pennsylvania woods. A bad shot in Alaska almost always means a lost ram.

I describe those months in the Alaska Range now as the most conflicted time of my life. I would spend seventy days testing myself in all the ways I love, moving through the Alaskan wilderness, a place of such power and vastness it is incomprehensible even to my memory. I watched a mama grizzly bear feed wild blueberries to her cubs, I woke to the footfall of a hungry-eyed silver wolf whispering through our campsite, I watched a bull moose rub the velvet off his bloody antlers, and a bald eagle dive for a parka squirrel. I watched the happy chaos that is a herd of caribou for hours, and the contrastingly calculated movements of the sheep for days.

I learned from the animals their wilderness survival skills, learned, of course, a few of my own. I learned, in those days, my place in the universe, learned why I need the wilderness, not why *we* need it, but why *I* do. That I need the opportunity to give in to something bigger than myself, like falling into love, something bigger, even, than I can define. This did not have to do with shooting an animal (though it would have, of course, in its purest form, had we not packages and packages of freeze-dried chicken stew) but with simpler skills: keeping warm in subzero temperatures, avoiding the grizzly bears that were everywhere and unpredictable, not panicking when the shale started shifting underneath my boot soles in a slide longer and steeper than anything I'd ever seen in the lower forty-eight, finally riding that shale slide out like a surfer on a giant gray wave.

I listened to the stories of the hunters, the precision and passion with which the best among them could bring the memories of past hunting camps to life. I understood that part of what we were about in hunting camp was making new stories, stories that were the closest these men ever got to something sacred, stories that would grace years, maybe even generations, of orange campfire light.

But underneath all that wonder and wildness and the telling of tales, the fact remains that in payment for my Alaskan experience I watched five of the most beautiful, smartest, and wildest animals I'd ever seen die, most of them slowly and in unspeakable pain. And regardless of the fact that it was the hunter who pulled the trigger, I was the party responsible for their deaths. And though I eat meat and wear leather, though I understand every ethical argument there is about hunting including the one that says it is hunters who will ultimately save the animals because it is the NRA who has the money and the power to protect what is left of America's wilderness, it will never be okay with me that I led my hunters to those animals. There is no amount of learning that can, in my heart, justify their deaths.

So when I remember that time in my life, I try to think not only of the killing but also of the hunting, which is a work of art, a feat of imagination, a flight of spirit and a test of endless patience and skill. To hunt an animal successfully you must think like an animal, move like an animal, climb to the top of the mountain just to go down the other side, and always be watching, and waiting, and watching. To hunt well is to be at once the hunter and the hunted, at once the pursuer and the object of pursuit. The process is circular, and female somehow, like giving birth, or dancing. A hunt at its best ought to look, from the air, like a carefully choreographed ballet.

French psychoanalyst Jacques Lacan believed that men desire the object of their desire, while women desire the condition of desiring, and this gives women a greater capacity for relishing the hunt. I believe that is why, in so many ancient and contemporary societies, women have been the superior hunters. Good hunting is no more about killing an animal than good sex is about making babies or good writing is about publication. The excitement, even the fulfillment, is in the beauty of the search. While a man tends to be linear about achieving a goal, a woman can be circular and spatial. She can move in many directions at once, she can be many things at once, she can see an object from all sides, and, when it is required, she is able to wait.

Occasionally there is a man who can do these things (most of the guides I knew were far better at them than I), and he is a pleasure to guide and to learn from. But the majority of my clients started out thinking that hunting is like war. They were impatient like a general, impatient like a sergeant who thinks he should be the general, impatient for the sound of his own gun and impatient for the opposition to make a mistake.

But the sheep didn't often make mistakes, and they were as patient as stone. So it was my job to show the hunter that he could choose a different metaphor. If hunting can be like war it can also be like opera, or fine wine. It can be like out-of-body travel, it can be like the suspension of disbelief. Hunting can be all of these things and more; like a woman, it won't sit down and be just one thing.

I wore a necklace in my hunting days, a bear claw of Navajo silver. The man I was in love with, the hunting guide, had given it to me to make amends for one of our breakups, one of his affairs. He gave it to me in a tiny box, wrapped elaborately, like a ring, and I shook it, heard it clunk, thought, Oh my God, Oh my God, he's really doing it. When I opened it, saw that it was not a ring but a pendant, I was not disappointed. I simply wore the pendant like a ring, confusing the symbolism of that pendant just enough to carry me back into the relationship, and back into hunting camp one last time.

It was late August, and much too warm in the high mountains. I'd been dropped, by airplane, one hundred air miles from Tok with two bow hunters from Mississippi. We'd made a base camp and climbed from it, up the valley of the Tok River to the glacial headlands. The sheep would stay high in the warm weather, higher, probably, than we could climb. But we tried anyway, crossing glacial rivers normally small but now raging in the heat wave, knowing after each crossing that we wouldn't make it back across until the weather turned again and the water began to subside. We had our packs, of course, a tent, sleeping bags, a change of clothes and enough food, if we didn't shoot anything, for a little better than three days.

When we got to the glacier at the head of the valley we hadn't seen any recent sheep sign, and this told us that the sheep would be higher still, lying with their bellies in a snowfield, not even needing to eat until the weather cooled down. We were wet and tired, hot and hungry, but we dropped half our gear, the tents and bedding, and climbed higher up the rocky moraine that flanked the glacier. We climbed through tangled forests of alder that grew, it seemed, horizontally out of the rocks, climbed over the soggy mounds of tundra, squeezing into it with our boot tips and fingernails when it got too steep. Our socks got wetter, our breathing more labored; for hours we climbed and still no sign of the sheep.

The hunters—I forget their names now, but let's just call them Larry and Moe—were nervous. We were all nervous. The packs were too heavy, the air was too thick, the sun was too hot, and we'd come too long and too far not to have seen any sign of the sheep. We collapsed on the top of a rocky outcropping surrounded by tundra. Larry amused himself by shooting arrow after arrow at a ptarmigan (a fat bird with fuzzy white après-ski boots on) who, as slow and stupid as that particular bird can be, let the arrows whizz by his head. Larry couldn't hit him, and the bird refused to fly away. Moe poked at a hole in the ground with a long stick, worrying whatever was inside. I went into my pack, looking for food, and found, buried between the cans of tuna and dried apricots, a rock—quartz, I believe—weighing six or seven pounds.

"You sons of bitches," I said to Larry and Moe, who had been watching me, smirking.

That's when the ground hornets finally got angry enough to come out of the hole in front of Moe. Maybe bees know who in a crowd is allergic to them; these bees seemed to. Four of them, anyway, came straight for me, and stung me on the hand. The first-aid kit, the shots of epinephrine, had made it as far as the mouth of the glacier and no farther, and that was at least four hours away.

I sat quietly and listened to my heartbeat quicken, my breathing accelerate into a frenzy. This is how it's all going to end, I thought, bee-stung, and trapped on the glacier with Larry and Moe. Then self-preservation took over. I ordered Larry to carry me on his back over to the glacier, ordered Moe to scout ahead and find a place where the ice had melted and the water had pooled. I tried to exert no energy as Larry climbed with me across the moraine and onto the glacier. Moe whistled that he had found a pool several inches deep, and Larry laid me in it while I did my best to breathe through the ever-smaller opening that was my throat.

I lay in that glacial pool until I was so numb I wasn't sure I could feel my torso. Eventually, the adrenaline subsided and my throat eased back open. My hand, my whole arm, was swollen to five or six times its normal size. I wrapped myself up in what remained of our dry clothes and tried to chew on a granola bar but I had no appetite. The late Alaskan summer night was bending on into evening, the sun rolling sideways along the horizon and threatening to go below it. It would get cold soon and the night wind off the glacier would start. No one wanted to say what we all knew: that we had to get back down to the mouth of the glacier by nightfall, had to get to our sleeping bags before it turned cold. Larry couldn't carry me the whole way, and I wondered, if I couldn't make the climb back down through the tundra and rock and alders to where our gear lay, would it be the right thing for them to simply leave me behind?

"Let's give it a try," I said. "If we go now we can go slowly." This wasn't true, but I spoke with authority and the boys believed me. We'd be climbing back through those alders at the worst time of day. Our range of vision would be cut way down, the rocks and tree trunks would be slippery with dew, and the grizzly bears would be moving. "You guys sing real loud now," I told them. "Let's give the bear the opportunity to do the right thing."

We moved across the tundra and back down into the alders.

With every step, every tightening of muscle, my arm exploded in pain and my head swam. My pulse increased, my throat tightened, and I had to drop back a little and rest until it began to open again. Eventually the fall got so steep and the alders so thick that there was nothing to do but lower ourselves through the branches with our arms, like children on a jungle gym. The pain in my arm reached a certain level of excruciation, and then moved on into numbness, the way a blister will if you keep walking long hours after it has popped. We could hear animals moving near us in the alder, big animals, and every now and then we'd get a whiff of dark musk.

"Sing louder, goddammit!" I shouted ahead to the boys, who were scared into silence by the noises beside them, and bent on getting back out in the open to the relative safety of the place on the glacier where we'd left the tent. They broke into a halfhearted round of "King of the Road," and I could tell by their voices they were moving much faster than I could, and would soon leave me out of screaming range.

That's when the heavy chain on which I wore my bear claw caught on an alder branch, just as I bent my elbows and swung my legs down to the next-lower set of branches, and my head snapped up and I was nearly hanged there, by the strength of that chain and the weakness of my arm and the force of gravity pulling me down. I gasped for breath, but there was none, and so I lifted my good arm up to the branch above me and did something I never could do in gym class, a one-handed chin-up, and repositioned my feet and unhooked my necklace from the alder branch.

I took the bear claw in the palm of my hand and felt the coolness of the silver, and I felt my strong heart pumping, sending blood to every part of my body, including my mis-shapen arm, and I realized I'd had it wrong all along about the necklace. That I had relied on somebody else's set of metaphors to understand it. That it had nothing to do, finally, with an engagement ring or the man who gave it to me, that it had, finally, nothing whatsoever to do with a man. And that whatever role that man had played in taking me to the Alaskan wilderness in the first place, he had nothing to do with why I stayed, nothing to do with all the things my seasons with the hunters, with the animals, had taught me, nothing whatsoever to do with the strength and tenacity that was getting me, bee-stung and frightened and freezing, down that near-dark Alaskan hill.

I wore the necklace differently after that, and years later, when the clasp on it wore paper-thin and the pendant fell one day into my coincidentally open hand, I replaced it with pieces of eight from the seventeenth century that I found near a silver mine in Bolivia, and I wait now to discover the meaning of this new/old silver I wear.

It's been years since I've guided any hunters, though I have returned to the Alaskan wilderness, with a camera or a kayak or a pair of cross-country skis. I am a far better outdoorsperson for my years guiding hunters, and even more important, I have a much deeper understanding of my animal self. I also have the blood of five fine and wild animals on my hands, and I will never forget it. And this is perhaps why, like the hunters, I need to keep telling my story, over and over again.

Dante
and Sally

Whenever I stop at the health food store I love to shop at, I come home with four giant organic beef bones, one for each of my four dogs. Being organic, these bones cost me $1.19 a pound, unless my favorite butcher, John, is working, and then I get them for free. John became my favorite butcher one day when I watched a woman throw the perfectly trimmed organic beef filet she had ordered back in his face when she found out it was going to cost sixty dollars. The math was simple, but apparently she hadn't done it. It was two days before Christmas, and the look on John's face as he held the piece of meat he had trimmed so lovingly turned me into Santa Claus.

"If you tell me how to cook that, I'll make it my Christmas dinner," I said, and his eyes lit right up.

"Tell me the truth," he said, holding it toward me. "Have you ever seen such a beautiful piece of meat?"

Since I was having only one guest for Christmas dinner, the dogs got a good bit of that $15.99-per-pound filet. With the exception of perfectly cared for elk loin steaks, it was the best meat I ever had, and it solidified my relationship with John, who now always updates me on Organic Meat News and gives me dog bones, always in multiples of four.

When I pull into the driveway four hours later (I live a long way from the nearest health food store), Sally and Dante come running out to greet me: Sally, the coyote/Australian shepherd mix, compact and athletic, the Mary Lou Retton of dogs; Dante, the Irish wolfhound, gangly and forty inches tall at the shoulder, limbs all akimbo, his gait half camel, half jackrabbit, very little dog. Hailey and Jackson, who are quite old and lame, are slower to acknowledge my arrival, but they, too, eventually hobble out to greet me.

Before I'm even out of the truck, Dante's nose is working. It's not that he isn't happy to see me. He is. And tonight we'll sleep in my queen-sized bed together in a position that I would be a little embarrassed for all but my closest friends to see. Nose to nose, heads on the pillow, his body prone and longer than mine, one foreleg thrown across my middle, one back leg thrown across my legs. I've never had a dog that wanted to cuddle quite this much, or quite this . . . humanly. But it is also true that Dante has a wider range of emotions than any man I dated during my twenties. I am grateful that he is only my dog. If he were my son I'd have doomed his future wives and girlfriends a hundred times over. What I'm saying is, if you look up *mama's boy* in the encyclopedia, there is a picture of Dante and me.

Right now, though, he's all business, because he knows that bones are part of this greeting ritual, and he's been ready for his since he heard my truck rumbling up the county road. I distribute the bones according to the old age-before-beauty rule:

the first one to Jackson, so blind and senile now that I have to put it right under his nose. The next one goes to Hailey, who still has all her faculties and has always been a girl who likes her treats. The third goes to Sally because she is a year older than Dante, and the last to the youngest and the largest dog.

Dante is the only dog I have ever had who did not come from a pet store or a pound. While Sally spent her first year foraging for garbage and small rodents on the Navajo reservation (the vet said he thought she'd never been handled by a human being), and Hailey was separated from her mother and dropped off at the Durango pound before she was three weeks old, and Jackson spent God knows how many weeks lying in a cage in a pet store with first one set of pedigreed dogs then another, Dante was happily ensconced with his wolfhound mother (pedigreed all the way back to Danny O'Hanion O'Donnell O'Dell in Ireland) and his fourteen wolfhound brothers and sisters with green grass and blue skies and all the designer puppy food he could eat.

And it shows. The other day I made soup that required using two veal shanks and when I was done with the bones there were only two to hand out. I gave one to Hailey because she'd gotten up on her rickety legs and walked across the difficult kitchen linoleum all by herself. I had the other bone in my hand, with both Sally and Dante clamoring at my heels. I decided, *May the best dog win*, and I hurled the bone out into the yard. Sally ran to grab it, but Dante didn't make a move off the porch. He sat and looked into my eyes expectantly, and I realized the difference between Dante and my other dogs.

Dante believes in a world where there will always be four bones.

When there is thunder and lightning at my house this is the situation: Jackson heads straight for the bathtub, Hailey wedges herself deep beneath the porch, Sally buries herself among the suitcases under my bed, and if she's outside when the storm starts she'll rip her way straight through a screen. And Dante will lie in the middle of the yard watching the flashes of light, hearing the thunder boom, as if the whole show were being put on expressly for him.

Dante gets the most attention of any dog on my ranch, but believes in his heart of hearts that he should get a little bit more. When I go away he is always sad, even if his very favorite dog-sitter is coming to stay with him. He can mope with the best of them. *Why can't we all just be here together all the time?* Watching him cycle through his mood swings over the course of a day can be as exhausting as living with a manic depressive. Content: *Oh, I'm in bed with my mom and I'm totally happy.* Conflicted: *Oh, I'm so comfortable here, but I have to go out to pee.* Wounded: *I had to go out to pee and now she won't let me in again and the sun just came up and I'm freezing.* Worried: *Mom's going to the car, but she didn't have any suitcases. Hailey, did you see any suitcases?* Perplexed: *What are the humans doing now?* Contentious: *I don't understand why there isn't enough rack of lamb for everyone.* Surly: *I don't get why the human gets more covers than me.* Mopey: *All she ever does is stare into that damn computer.* Excited: *We're going for a walk, hey come on, Sally, we're walking with Mom, I hope we go all the way to the river.* Relieved: *That's Mom's car, I know that's Mom's car, I wonder if she brought bones.*

Personally, I can't relate to Dante's idyllic upbringing, and I have tended to live my life a little more like Sally, who fights for every bone like it's the last one that might ever be offered, and who thinks every time we put her in the car it's because we are going to drop her off somewhere on the side of the road.

"Has anything bad ever happened when we get in the car?" my friend David says each time to Sally, but she just pants harder and tries to shove her whole body farther under the seat.

I don't know what happened to Sally before I got her, but I do know that her reactions to anything that reminds her of that dark place are strong and involuntary. I know that no matter how many years she spends in the near perfect safety of this ranch, she will never get over it. There will always be the lightning and thunder to remind her.

Sometimes Sally and I sit together and watch Dante move through the world in all his innocent entitlement and I feel just the shadow of a memory of a time—it must have been so early—before all the bad things started to happen to me. I think maybe Sally sees it too, and remembers. I think that's why she lets Dante drag her around the yard, her back leg in his mouth, not hard enough to hurt, just playful. I think that's why, though she is less than half his size, she always tries to put herself between him and another dog. Like me, she is determined to preserve that perfect innocence in him as long as is caninely possible. Like me, she is hoping that his innocence will connect her to her own.

A writing student of mine called not too long ago—I'll call her Patti—and said she was in the neighborhood and would like to drop by. I live four hours from the nearest health food store, ninety miles from the nearest market. Here, no one is ever in the neighborhood. If you're in my neighborhood, you came a long damn way.

Nevertheless and in spite of my better judgment I invited her for dinner, which this far from anywhere also means for the night. David and I had to get up at five in the morning to drive to Denver, and were planning an early night. Patti is a drinker, which scares me generally, but especially on a night when I have to be the one to call lights out.

She arrived, and for a while things went along swimmingly. David made Salad Niçoise. Patti opened and drank almost all of a bottle of wine.

Then she said:

"I brought my dog because I'm dying for you to meet him. If it's okay with you I'll let him out of the truck."

The dog's name was Attila. That should have been my first clue. But then Patti said:

"Your dogs aren't aggressive, are they?"

After twenty years of dog ownership, I know that when someone asks if your dog is aggressive it means, without exception, that theirs is. But I still didn't catch on.

"No," I said, "not in the least. Jackson used to be, but he's blind and deaf and his fighting days are over. Dante wouldn't hurt a fly."

Patti let Attila the Rottweiler out of the car and it didn't take a second for him to run over to Dante, grab him by the soft fleshy part of his foreleg, and rip into it with his teeth. Dante never knew what hit him; he rolled over, totally submissive, and let Attila bite right through one of his legs and then another. Sally was there first, snarling and spitting at Attila, but he didn't even hear her.

I screamed bloody murder and kicked Attila in the head until he finally let go. I took Dante into the kitchen and he fell into a quivering mass on the floor. David got on the phone to the veterinarian. Patti opened her second bottle of wine. I lay on the floor with Dante, petting him and cooing to him and trying to get him to stop shaking.

David was writing down things that the vet said about canine saliva glands and infections. Patti, more than a little drunk now, kept saying that everything would be okay if we just let Attila in. Outside the window his eyes glowed yellow and every few minutes he lunged at the glass and Dante went into another round of the shakes.

David said the vet wanted to see Dante first thing in the morning, then he proceeded to do what he does best: walk around the kitchen and try to normalize things. "Dogs will be dogs," he said, and I wanted to kill him.

"I've seen him do a lot more damage than that," Patti said. Attila lurched at the window again, and I choked out my first words in a half hour.

"I want you to lock that dog up in your truck."

Patti was beside herself now, insisting that I would really like Attila if I just got to know him, if I would just give him what he wanted and let him in the house. When I couldn't stand the sound of her voice anymore I left her and David to play the whole thing down together, and I took my scared and wounded Dante to bed.

David found me an hour later, balled up and sobbing. Dante would be a different dog now, I wailed. It was our job to protect him and we had failed. What the hell kind of a dog mother was I, I sobbed, to sit back and let such a thing happen.

When David did his best to comfort me I turned on him. What kind of man, I wanted to know, would allow a monster like that in his house. Never mind that technically speaking it was my house. Never mind that David had nothing to do with my telling Patti she could come. Lucky for me, David makes allowances when I occasionally go out of my head.

It was 2:00 a.m. and I was still sobbing when I heard the sound of a dog fight. I flew out of the house in my underwear to find Attila, who had somehow squeezed his 110-pound frame out of six inches of open truck window and had pounced—this time—on Jackson.

Guest or not, Rottweiler or not, I was way out of patience. I pulled Attila off of Jackson by his collar, and more or less drop-kicked him across the yard. When I led a very disoriented Jackson into the mudroom to check for damages, he appeared unscathed—through his mass of blond dreadlocks it was hard to tell for sure—and he actually seemed rather invigorated by the encounter. He strutted his arthritic three-legged walk in circles around the mudroom, coughing up phlegm and ready for more. *Yeah, you and three of your friends next time, buddy*, he was saying. I gave him some dog food and knocked on the guest-room door.

I found Patti sitting up in bed working on her third bottle of wine. What I wonder now is why I didn't kick her out then and there. But I went back to my room and lay wide awake listening to both David and Dante snoring, listening to the clink of Patti's wineglass and wanting somebody to kill.

A few hours later the sun rose and Patti left and Doc Howard fixed Dante up with antibiotics and a little doggie wound drain. My friend Charlotte promised to come out and stay with him for the twenty-four hours David and I would be gone.

As it turned out, the incident with Attila doesn't seem to have changed Dante at all. He still rolls over for every new dog, still sits outside during thunderstorms, still expects more than his share of attention, still seems to believe that the world exists mostly to give him and his friend Sally a beautiful place to play. Maybe a happy puppyhood is as hard to rattle as a traumatic one is to get over. That's what Sally told me, anyway, and she ought to know.

Dante's lying at my feet as I finish this. The mood is Petulant: *I thought you said that you and I were going to have some quality time tonight.* I'm going to shut the computer off in a minute and take him to bed and rub his ears until he's sleeping. Dante believes in a world where there will always be four dog bones, and it is my job as dog mother to keep it that way.

mountains
and rivers

———————

A River Runs
Through Them

Day One: Looking like beekeepers in floppy hats and mosquito netting, long pants and long sleeves, the urbanites will arrive at the put-in, arms full of gear, most of which the guide's letter told them to leave at home: one carefully washed and pressed T-shirt for each day, brand-new Teva sandals, still hooked together with a small plastic twistee, and, in the case of both the stockbroker and the literary agent, a tiny cellular phone.

Although the dermatologist from the Twin Cities will assure them that after No. 15 it's all the same, they will each wear three bottles of sunscreen around their necks with numbers ranging from 24 to 65. Given their choice, the women will all get into one boat, the men in another. The boats will maintain this junior-high-school-dance configuration an astonishing 80 percent of the time.

The guide will name the ever deepening rock layers in the canyon walls, explain the various stages of desert varnish, point out cacti—prickly pear, barrel, and hedgehog—and find a group of desert bighorn ewes and lambs. The passengers will only want to know about the rapids: when will they get to them, how bad are they really, is it true that last year somebody died?

Despite the heat, nobody will jump into the water on the first day: there are too many clothes to be taken off and put on, and they are afraid they will look ungraceful trying to get back into the boat. They will be ashen-faced and cottonmouthed in the small opening rapids where the guide will assure them she couldn't flip the boat even if she tried.

By the time they get to camp, the acupuncturist, the infectious disease specialist, and the guy who will only say he's "in oil" will all be sunburnt, and the ex–poet laureate of the United States will have been stung by a bee. Three hats will have gone overboard, one pair of Tevas will have been left at the lunch spot, and at least one of the vegetarians will be hungry enough to eat meat.

Over dinner (orange roughy Mexicana, fresh asparagus, parsley new potatoes, and Bear Lake raspberries with real whipped cream), they will each tell the story of the last time they slept on the ground. The guide will look at the cloudless night sky and suggest sleeping under the stars. There will be urgent whispering about snakes, scorpions, and rain. The tents will be pitched, and before bed the guide will give a lesson about finding their way by constellation.

By day two they will have realized several things: that they really do have to shit in something called a "rocket box," that there aren't many mosquitoes in the desert after all, and that it probably would have been okay to sleep outside. The beekeeping nets will be packed away, and most people will have traded long pants for bathing suits, long-sleeved shirts for

Bain de Soleil. The clinical psychologist from Chicago will make the first splash, and before lunch everybody will have had a life-jacketed swim through a minor rapid.

They will have exhausted the surface information about each other's lives and will begin to ask questions about the things they see. After dinner (barbecued chicken, fresh spinach, corn on the cob, and pineapple upside-down cake), the ex–Flying Tiger will drink just enough rum to tell everyone about what happens when he travels in space and time.

By day three they will realize there is no point in trying to get their fingernails clean, that washing dishes is the best job (momentarily clean hands), and that closing up the toilet after everyone has finished is the worst. They will realize that swimming in the silty river makes them feel a little dirtier than before they went in, that everybody's hair gets greasy in three days, but not equally, and the two Berkeley computer guys, unshaven, will start to wear bandannas around their heads and look like members of a gang. The rapids will get bigger and bigger, and they will realize that when the guide says she thinks they should zip up their life jackets for this one, she means it.

By this time, everybody will know the difference between a cliff swallow and a sandpiper. Geology will have stopped being just the title of one of the sections of the guidebook and will have started to mean time and wind and water; they will see it all there in the record of the rock. They will notice the way the sunlight colors the canyon differently, every hour from the time the sun rises until the time it sets. In the morning the talk will be about opera, deconstruction, monogamy; the time traveler will admit that the planetary federation on Venus was supporting Ross Perot.

By late afternoon they will have figured out it's okay to be quiet, and they will drift through miles of deepening canyon without a word, or cough, or laugh. Tonight there won't even be talk of setting up tents. The military policeman and the Hungarian film producer will begin a joyous, clandestine affair and will fool no one. After dinner (linguine with clam sauce, salad, dutch oven brownies) *they* will show the guide which star points north.

On day four they will run the biggest rapid of the trip, and something will happen to somebody that makes it seem to them that they all almost died. What will follow this is a lot of serious discussion about making the most of their time, about how fragile they all are, about how being outside puts them in touch with some essential part of themselves. They will start planning which river they want to float next year, they will speculate about what it would cost for a cabin and a couple of acres in the area, and when the guide tells them they will say, always, "Damn, I pay more than that to park my car."

By now they are turning a nice rusty river color. They are forgetting, in the morning, to change into their carefully packed shirts. It's hard to keep them in the boats, in and out like seals all day long, burned and peeling and burning again. They will begin to say things like "Coming out here has made me like myself again," and "It's amazing how much living in the city makes you forget." They will say, "This is so very beautiful," they will say, "My God, the things I've missed."

By the fifth day, they will start seeing literary shapes in the rock formations—there's Don Quixote and Sancho Panza; there's George Jetson's dog Astro; there's Roddy McDowell as he appeared in *Planet of the Apes*. Fear long gone, they will whoop and holler in the rapids, and say, "Wow! Please, can't we go back up and do that again?"

When they stop for the night, the stockbroker, the shamanic healer, and the actress will work together like a chain gang unloading gear. The psychologist and the computer brothers will have the kitchen assembled and the salad made before the guide finishes pumping water out of her boat. It's the last night on the river, and they won't even be talking about showers anymore; they want, they will say, the trip to go on forever.

They will emerge from the canyon and arrive at the take-out by noon on the sixth day. They will stand between the deflating boats and the running bus that will take them back to their rent-a-cars like so many Persephones, the pomegranate bitten, both worlds beckoning, neither enough. There will be more hugging than anyone would have anticipated after only five days.

The guide will thank them for their hard work and good company. She will tell them that nearly every wild river in the world is threatened by something: power plants, pollution, drought, development, irrigation, recreation, corruption, greed. She will hope that they will carry whatever piece of themselves they found on the river back to the cities with them. She will hope they will make decisions that will keep the rivers flowing for the time when they want to come again.

The Pit Bull and
the Mountain Goat

I remember the first time I drove into Park City. It was ten
years ago next September, the day was cool and sunny, the
sky from horizon to horizon a shade I've since come to think of
as Utah blue. I noticed Osgood Thorpe's Dairy Barn first, the
whitewashed sideboards and weather vanes, and the ocean of
fields he owned around it. Behind the barn was a mountain of
aspen trees, nearly all gone yellow, and the scrub oak, glowing
red, and the evergreens. Snaking down the mountain and
through the trees were the ski runs: Prospector, King Consoli-
dated, Glory Hole, Pay Day, runs I would ski so many times in
the next ten years I'd forget that their names referred to anything besides steeps and bumps and fresh Utah powder. I'd forget that in those names lay the reason Park City was built in the
first place: silver mines and the men who worked them. It took
me about five minutes to fall in love with their ramshackle Vic-
torian houses and the rickety stairways they built to climb the
canyon walls between them, the abandoned mine shafts and the
stained-glass windows, the old whorehouse and the train station, and all the other ghosts the miners had left behind.

I'd been living in Salt Lake City, under the inversion layer and the eyes of my Mormon neighbors, having signed on to a five-year Ph.D. program at the University of Utah. My teachers and colleagues said if I moved to Park City all I'd do is ski and drink and sit in the sun and walk in the mountains. They said I'd stop coming to classes, stop writing papers, I probably wouldn't even get my degree. All I knew was that the air was clean and you could see all the stars at night, and every house I looked at had a path out the back where you could put on your skis and ski right down to the town lift.

I rented a hundred-year-old house straight out of Munchkinland with no insulation, doorways I had to duck to get through, and floors that sloped a different direction in every room down and away from some high point in the center. When the snow and ice slid off the tin roof it made a noise that had me swearing the house was splitting down the middle, as it will one day soon I'm sure. I learned to cook with the woodstove that the house had been built around in 1898, and I dug bottles out of my garden that were handmade from thick colored glass and stamped, like money. My neighbor across the street was the genuine article, an ancient miner who hooked himself up to an oxygen tank for four hours every day to fight the silicosis in his lungs. He fell in love with my dog Hailey and fed her white bread and fried chicken even after I told him the vet forbade it. I took long walks with the dogs all over the mountain, learning the names of the ski runs, standing on the fall lines, willing it to snow.

My life became enormously uncomplicated in Park City. I would get up when the sun hit my bedroom window, which was around six in the summer and eight in the winter and not at all on those very few days a year when the sun didn't shine. I would write until I got bored with myself, and then walk down to the Morning Ray for coffee and muffins, and then on down Main Street to the post office. I would stop by and pet the cat at Dolly's bookstore, and visit Peter Snosnowski who cuts my hair, and then I'd walk back up the hill and go to work.

When the snow started to fall and the lifts opened I was out there every morning, carving fresh turns down Assessment, Powder Keg, and Blue Slip Bowl. I didn't take Utah snow for granted in those days, and each morning the feathery arcs my skis kicked up seemed like brand-new miracles, the soundless weightless sensation of moving through snow that came all the way across a desert to fall in my backyard. If it wasn't a powder day there'd be a better-than-even chance I'd make it to my literature class. Sometimes I didn't move my truck for several days at a time.

I remember that first year on the mountain, the uncrowded December days, where I'd pick one chairlift a day and ski all the runs till I had them memorized: the trees on the left of Thaynes Run kept the bumps soft there until late in the day, but the Hoist was where the real bump skiers carved the best lines. I remember my first day up into Jupiter Bowl, Park City's lift-accessed expert-only terrain, my first tentative turns down the West Face on an early powder day watching for stumps and rocks, and then the first moment of letting go, of giving my weight to the mountain. I remember the first time I hiked to the top of Scott's Bowl, the highest accessible point on the mountain, the first time I let my skis drop off its big cornice, the feeling of landing in something not quite bottomless, but a very long way from solid ground. I remember my first time in the steeper MacConkey's Bowl, scared and back so far on my skis I snapped the buckle off my boot, missed a turn, and tumbled five hundred vertical feet before I came to rest, skiless and poleless with one boot halfway off, but whole and grinning like a cartoon snow creature at my friends' enthusiastic round of applause.

I came to love Scott's Bowl the best; though I never got very good at skiing it, I loved to stand at the top of it and look out at the whole Wasatch Front stretched before me in one direction, and the wetland meadows where the sandhill cranes made their homes in the other, at Mount Timpanogos, the sleeping princess, behind me, and everywhere acres of untracked snow. I loved the drop off the cornice, the turns down the face which was the perfect amount of steep, for powder, for crud, for me. I loved knowing I had the long trip to the base ahead of me, loved knowing how easy the groomers would feel after skiing the bowl, how soft and immaculate Silver Queen would be, how fast I could take the last turn (the only turn) down Nastar.

I learned that first year too the legends of Park City, not just the legends of the old days and the silver boom, but the new ones the young town was creating. There was Dan McCann, for instance, the best skier and mountaineer in town, who amazed everyone by being the first man to climb and ski 12,800 feet of Mount Timpanogos, all in one short winter day. The best bar in town then was Cisero's basement, on Wednesday, jam night, though any of the rugby players would tell you it was the Alamo, and they ought to know, being legendary themselves. The best meal in town was at Adolph's, if you could afford it, and if you couldn't the best deal was back at Cisero's, locals' spaghetti night, all you could eat for $5.95. Most people agreed that the best-looking men in town were the Peek brothers, who did carpentry out of the backs of their pickup trucks and occasionally put the money together to buy, refurbish, and sell a house. The best cup of coffee was and always will be at the Morning Ray. The best day of the year back then was Clown Day, April 1, when all the locals dressed as clowns and ate mushrooms and skied their brains out in the perfect spring corn snow, pushing the bumps aside as they went, giggling their heads off. The best nights were in the off season when there was no work and even less money, and we'd gather on porches to tell stories and sing and play guitar.

The off season was a good time to get up high in the mountains too, and after almost ten years of driving through the Heber Valley and looking up at Mount Timpanogos—of studying the figure of the sleeping princess, of waiting for the first autumn morning when she is dusted in snow, of watching the snowfield on the northeasternmost slope melt into the horse's head that signals the planting of corn in the valley— after years of more or less worshiping that mountain, I finally took the time to climb it. I was with my oldest friend, Kelly, who lives in Chicago, and who was thinking of making the big move out west.

I took her up Timpanogos because I wanted to show her how easy it is for us to get into the wilderness, how it's right there in our backyards whenever we need it, how sometimes we don't realize we need it until we are there. But halfway up the trail I thought I had made a mistake. First there was the graffiti, scrawled across every sign and available rock, and when we started to climb, every switchback had been crosscut two or three times; on the flat parts eight or sometimes ten trails reached across the meadows.

In a western state where a relatively small percentage of the population actually goes hiking, the damage I saw was staggering. I was ashamed of the way that trail had been treated, ashamed that I had taken Kelly to a place not pristine at all, but scarred and ugly. I was working up an apology, some way of convincing her that not all the trails in Utah are like this, when she said, "This is absolutely the most incredibly beautiful place I have ever seen in my life."

And when I lifted my head and looked more than ten feet beyond my hiking boots, I knew, of course, that she was right. There we were, in a massive glacial cirque, surrounded on three sides by vertical granite walls, and on the fourth by more wildflowers than the average Chicagoan could ever dream of: Indian paintbrush, every shade from the palest yellow through the oranges and into the deepest red; purple fireweed; white, pink, and multicolored columbine; lavender bluebells. Beyond the flowers stood the rest of the Wasatch Mountains, and beyond those, the high Uintas. I was busy looking at outhouse trails and boot marks while all around me was the definition of sublime.

After another couple of hours of climbing, Kelly and I arrived at the top of Timpanogos—at the funny little metal house that must have been important to someone—and sat down for a drink. We got our first real look down the populated side of the mountain, and there was Orem spread below us, with its belching smokestacks, and Provo, at rush hour in fact, traffic all backed up along Interstate 15. We heard car horns blowing clear as a bell even there where we sat, almost eight thousand feet above them. We watched a golden eagle make lazy circles between us and the city, and I stirred up some coyote scat that lay on the trail in front of me and wondered what could possibly live up this high on the windy, barren face of the mountain that a coyote would come all this way to eat. That's when I saw the sunlight catch the flash of two pointy black horns, and the bushy white back end of an animal moved behind a rock not three hundred feet in front of me.

"Did you see that?" I said to Kelly. But she shook her head.

"I know this sounds crazy," I said, "but I swear I just saw a mountain goat, not ten feet from the trail where we just climbed."

We watched and waited until the patriarch wandered back into our view. He was a big ram, an old ram, and we watched him settle his big body down in a small rock niche overlooking the smokestacks and traffic patterns, overlooking the smog.

"I can't believe it," I said to Kelly. "Of all the places, why would those goats want to live here?"

Mountain goats are shy creatures who, given the option, like to live in places where people don't ever go, and I was thinking about all the hikers, the dogs and children, who traverse the trail daily. I was thinking about the horse-pack trips, the train whistles and fire sirens, the fact that of all the trails in Utah, Timpanogos was probably the most heavily used.

"He probably likes the lights," Kelly said quietly. "At night the city lights must be awesome from up here."

We looked around the green meadow immediately below and realized we were surrounded by mountain goats, at least twenty ewes and lambs. While we were watching the ram, they had all come out to graze, and we watched for a long time, their white coats catching the setting sunlight, the city lights down below.

Kelly and I got off the mountain way too late that night—so late, in fact, that we had to hold hands and feel our way down the switchbacks in the dark, so late that my roommate had Search and Rescue halfway up the mountain before we could get to a phone and say we had made it just fine. Kelly was long gone back to Chicago before I understood why we had sat there so long watching the mountain goats when we knew we had six miles to hike back to the car.

It had to do with Park City, and the complaining we'd all been doing about the changes that had come on our town too fast and furious to comprehend. We sat in our cars out on Highway 224 all summer breathing each other's exhaust, eye to eye with a manhole cover, trying to imagine driving the new road, wide and high above the valley, no longer getting a feel for the lay of the land. We watched the construction of one big concrete structure after another as if they were mirages, remembering the sandhill cranes that used to migrate through those meadows, wondering what store we needed that we had lived so long without.

A new Wal-Mart opens up in America every two days. We were bound to get one eventually. Still, we felt somehow different from the rest of America, and in our difference we thought we were immune. We weren't. And it was difficult to count the ways all the development affected us. We didn't recognize anybody at the Albertsons anymore. And who were those people in their new Ford Explorers who didn't even smile and wave? We had our mountain bikes/tape decks/Ray-Bans stolen, and that would have never happened two or six or ten years ago. We were moaning about rental prices, but we'd all worked for less than ten dollars an hour forever, and who had the money to buy? Our years of hoping we wouldn't become another Aspen were behind us; for better or worse, Park City had arrived.

This was what we deserved, our yuppie siblings and disapproving parents told us, for living the way we did; and now, having seen Park City through its fledgling years, there was nothing to do except move on to some other town, where rent was cheap and work was plentiful and we could start all over again. Unless, of course, we were too stubborn to leave. Unless we looked at the fact that we had spent most of our adult lives making a home here and we were invested in saving the things about Park City that would allow us to stay.

We came here, many of us, in our twenties, when everything we owned fit into the back of a Honda Civic, and now we'd need Allied Van Lines to cart it away. We were attached to Park City in ways we'd never fully comprehend until we moved. In so many important respects we grew up here, and when I saw that goat hovering on the thin ridge of mountain between Sundance and Provo, I decided I wouldn't give up on Park City without a fight. I decided that if I could always see the wildflowers I could learn to love the city lights, and that was enough to keep me here, for a while.

I found out a few days after our hike that the mountain goats were introduced successfully onto Mount Timpanogos in 1981, the year before I first came to Utah, and that they have been thriving there ever since. A few days after that I heard another story about the goats that bears repeating.

A friend of mine named Ben went up Timpanogos with a backpack to spend the night near the windy summit. When he got there, he met another man, also making camp for the night, who had brought a pit bull with him up the trail. The two men set up camp about a half mile away from each other, and at dusk, when the goats came out to graze, Ben watched the other man sic his pit bull on the old patriarch, saying, "Kill! Kill!"—the command for the pit bull to lock his jaws.

Ben knew the man was carrying a bottle of Jack Daniel's, and not one but two pistols, but he moved forward anyway to try to intervene. He'd only got within swinging distance of the man with the guns when he saw what the goat was doing. Like some kind of Asian fan dancer the goat would lower his horns and pull the dog closer and closer to the edge of the cliff, waiting a little longer to jump sideways or upwards to the next rock ledge each time the dog lunged. The dog got more and more excited, less and less sensible, until finally the goat waited just long enough to send the dog hurtling seven hundred feet over the cliff.

Ben watched while the man climbed down and retrieved his dog, while he carried the dog's bloody body back to his camp. The dog was still alive then, and Ben asked if there was anything he could do to help, but the dog owner said the dog would be fine, and Ben went back to his tent alone. By the next morning the whiskey bottle was empty, the man was gone, and the dog was dead.

I spent the year after the Timpanogos hike living and teaching in Ohio in a place where the Wal-Mart-to-wilderness ratio is about a thousand to one. I walked—and I really believe this—every hiking trail in Ohio. None of them took more than half a day; all of them wound up in somebody's backyard. And what did I trade for the wilderness? I was forty-five minutes from a decent bookstore, an hour from an interesting restaurant, three hours from a professional sports team of any kind, and sixteen hundred miles from any snow worth skiing. I couldn't get a good cup of coffee, I couldn't buy Pepperidge Farm cookies at the grocery store, there was no such thing as Mexican food, and the most complicated movie I could see without driving a long way was *Honey I Shrunk the Kids*.

I missed Park City so badly that year that I even missed the things I don't like. I got sentimental about standing in line at the post office; my heart would race when I heard Orrin Hatch's name on TV. And all those things I thought I'd be so happy to get away from—the Christmas-week lift lines and the 5:00 a.m. trips to the Albertsons—seemed like awfully small reasons to move away.

I'm not saying I could accept the changes that were coming to Park City, any more than I could accept the way people had trashed the Timpanogos trail, and I'm sure even then I could see the time coming when I'd give up on Park City for good. But the trip to Ohio reminded me to look beyond my own hiking boots, to not lose sight of the things that were still good in Park City, things I knew we would have to keep track of, or we were bound to lose them too.

Like the way it feels that first day in November when the kind of snowflakes start to fall that make me say, "Tune the skis; we're hiking up to Jupiter tomorrow." Like the particular blue of an early April sky when I'm coming down Prospector face all alone, pushing the soft bumps out of my way as I go.

Like the fireworks exploding through the Thanksgiving snowflakes while the band America sings my high school prom theme for the hundred millionth time. Like Christmas week when we are all almost too burned out to be civil to one another, but we manage to come together, sometime between when the bars close and the lifts open, to decorate the tree and toast the new year. Like the summer symphony at Deer Valley, drinking wine and watching night fall on the forest while a hundred violinists play "Carolina in the Pines." Those are the times when I thought, "This is my town, and it's the best place I will ever be."

And if there was a lesson to be learned from the story of the pit bull, surely it lay in the tenacity of the goat. A goat who continued to hang in there, in spite of pollution, of traffic, of car horns, and one sick man with a pit bull. Like almost all of us, that goat was a transplant, and he must have known it could be worse; if he couldn't work it out on Timpanogos, he might have wound up in Ohio. He was a goat who learned to roll with the changes, and more important, maybe, he learned that—locking jaws notwithstanding—he was a smart enough goat to drive a pit bull over a cliff.

But Park City has changed a lot even since the day I saw the goats on Timpanogos, and I'm not as tenacious as they are, even though I might like to be. Tasteful, modern Victorian-look condos have replaced too many of the old crumbling houses. We got a K-Mart to go with our Wal-Mart and a mall full of outlet stores has made it impossible for even the most enterprising sandhill crane to land. I don't find any more old glass bottles or five-cent Campbell's soup cans when I go walking with the dogs. The back of every ski pass in Park

City now reads "Full and midweek season passes are not valid on April 1 or any other day when a season pass holder is dressed or made up as a clown," and most people who hold season passes these days have no idea why. The miner across the street died five years ago, but his angry wife still comes through for Hailey. "Come here, you son of a bitch," she screams out her front door, and Hailey waggles over and takes an entire loaf of three-day-old Wonder bread in her mouth. Osgood Thorpe's barn still stands, though the million-dollar houses are encroaching. Rumor has it that it took years and a big pile of money before he sold the county enough property to widen the last stretch of the road.

I know people who wind up leaving a place they've lived in a long time because they say they've outgrown it. But I'm leaving Park City because it's outgrown me. In the ten years I've been in Park City its population has increased 500 percent. The Morning Ray is three times its original size, the Peek brothers are millionaires, Peter has his own salon now and calls himself Peter Anthony, Dolly's burnt down and has been rebuilt, and they have a brand-new cat that sits in the window. We have espresso now, and sushi, and bars with bands that are actually worth paying money to see. We have fine art in the galleries and clothes from four continents and twenty-four-hour taxis and Federal Express. Park City is a world-class resort now; it's me who's still a little rough around the edges, and I'm bound to find someplace new that's at least as scruffy as I am.

I leave Park City grateful for my years there, for the comfort I found in a place whose every nook and cranny became as familiar to me as drawing a breath. My teachers were right, of course. I never did finish my Ph.D. But I did learn something anyway about what's important in my life: a stand of aspen trees, still green but just about to go golden, and first turns on a bright blue morning after the high desert angels have been making powder all night.

Powerhouse
by the Book

I n the eastern half of the United States, the average whitewater river trip takes five hours; in the Rockies, the average whitewater river trip takes five days. This is one of my
standard answers to the question of why I make my home in
the west, why I choose to live in a place without films or good
coffee, a place where the state population roughly equals the
number of square miles. I like living in a place where towns
are connected not by road, but by a river, a place where the
post office can't guarantee overnight delivery to anywhere, a
place where if you run out of gas, it can be a really big deal. I
like living in a place that has a one-and-a-quarter-million-acre
wilderness. And what I like best of all is to take my 15'6"
Achilles inflatable six-man rubber raft down the Middle Fork
of the Salmon River as it falls three thousand feet from
Boundary Creek to the Main Salmon through the rich green
heart of all that wild land.

The Middle Fork of the Salmon is my river of choice, not
only because it is the most pristine river corridor of any com-
mercially run river in America. Not only because of the dozen

or so hot springs that offer tired oarsmen a soak, one that shoots out from a fissure in the rock like a shower. Not only because of the wild life: Rocky Mountain bighorn rams and golden eagles on every trip, black bear and mountain goat and elk when we're lucky. Not only for the towering pine forests, the icy white side streams, the cornflower-blue sky. I would choose the Middle Fork solely and simply because of the white water, 341 rapids in five adrenaline-pounding heart-stopping days, more exciting and varied river running over a more extended stretch of river than any of the thirty-odd rivers I've run in America.

When I run the Middle Fork, which I try to do once a year, I want exactly two other people in my boat. One to do the constant bailing, and one to read the Handbook (a waterproof, detailed, and absolutely essential description of every rapid). I'll only take people who've been rafting with me before, who I can trust to keep their head when things get exciting. More than two people and my boat becomes heavy, sluggish, and maneuverability is the key to rafting the high-speed obstacle course called the Middle Fork.

The Middle Fork divides itself up in my mind by its seven class IV rapids that at high water turn into class Vs: Velvet Falls, Powerhouse, Pistol Creek, Tappen Falls, Redside, Weber, and Rubber Rapid. (Rapids are rated, universally, on a scale of I to VI. In classes I–III, if a boatman reads the water correctly, he can use the force of the river to help him get where he needs to be. In classes IV-V the river works against him, tries to drive him over steep falls, into sharp rocks, tries to tear the underside of his boat or flip it over. A class VI rapid means certain damage to life and property.) Getting through these seven monsters safe and topside will become both the focus and the rhythm of the trip.

It's a perfect Middle Fork morning, cool and clear, the sun sparkling off the surface of the water like sapphires, not a hint of a cloud in the sky. It's June and there's more water coming out of the Sawtooth Mountains than there has been at any other time in the last ten years. I've got my crew ready: John, a writer and horse packer from Colorado, will do the bailing; Kris, a lawyer turned ski-town swimming instructor, will read the Handbook.

On the chart at the ranger station we see that the river's running well above what the Forest Service calls a "normal, safe flow," and just below the red zone marked "too danger-ous to run safely." We're in a mixed-message gray area labeled "Hazardous—experienced boatmen only," and I wonder, as I always do just before I get behind the oars on a swollen river, how much experience is experience enough.

There is a buzzing at the launch site (a hundred-foot wooden ramp that boaters lower their rafts down with ropes, pulley-style, to the whitewater chaos below) as the twenty-odd people who make up today's three launches ready their boats. There is a churning that lets the passengers know this is not a southern Utah booze cruise, that this river has a one-in-four-thousand fatality rate, that at least a few people die on this river every year, most of them at this level.

We rig the boats carefully against flipping, tying and dou-ble-tying everything down with thick straps, get a late-morn-ing start, and roll and bump through the first five miles and thirty rapids (one continuous stretch of white water at this level) unharmed and confident. My boat is rigged with one set of twelve-foot oars in the center and I run most rapids facing forward, rowing upstream to slow the boat, so that I have more time to make the series of moves I need to make in each rapid.

"'Velvet Falls has a tendency to sneak up on the careless drifter,'" Kris reads from the Handbook. "'It has taken many boats unexpectedly and there have been several drownings at this location.'"

I'm not worried about Velvet sneaking up on me; what I'm worried about is what I know I have to do once I get to the edge of the rapid: pull my boat hard left and upstream, pull out of the current and move sideways and backwards, tucking in behind a huge boulder that takes up most of the left half of the river, the boulder that quiets the far left side of the rapid, the boulder that makes Velvet Falls both difficult and possible to run.

We pull over well above Velvet and sidestep along the mountain to scout it. The run is just like I remember from last year, only narrower, more water thundering around the thinner left-hand line, much less margin for error.

We get back in the boat and into the midstream current that's humping toward Velvet's big drop, the roar of the falls loud and mingling with the thumping of my own heart. I'm rowing upstream as fast and as hard as I can, but gaining little ground against the insistent river. The front of the boat noses the drop-off, and I see Kris's eyes get big because we are considerably right of where we need to be, certain to flip when we hit the wave at the bottom. We achieve a kind of cartoonesque suspension on the lip of the rapid, and then the big boat starts to respond to my rowing. We tuck neatly in behind the boulder and run the smooth water chute just below it dead straight and even.

In the picture in the Handbook, Powerhouse Rapid looks much less threatening than Velvet Falls. What the picture in the book can't measure is its length, half a mile of holes and walls and teethy boulders. You have to keep doing everything right for a long time.

John is bailing every drop out of the raft as we approach it, so I don't have to drag more weight than I need to through this obstacle course.

"Okay," I say to Kris, "let me have it."

" 'Enter just to the left of the midstream submerged boulders,' " Kris begins. " 'Maintain a position twenty feet off the left bank for the first hundred yards. Once past the boulder bar located on the right, pull hard to the right to avoid shallows on the left half of the river. Pass within three feet of the island at the lower end to avoid a very dangerous submerged boulder that is an extreme hazard at low water flows.' "

This is the language of scripture. Was that three feet to the left or the right of the island? "Read it again," I tell her, "from the shallows on."

" 'Maintain a midstream position when passing the rock wall on the right, located thirty feet below the island. Avoid a large submerged boulder by passing to its left fifty yards below the boulder bar. Once committed to the final drop, pull hard to the left to avoid a sheer rock wall and strong hydraulics on the right as the current forces you into the rock wall.' "

"Read it again," I tell her, as we pass the snaggletooth rock with six inches to spare, water crashing into the boat, the current churning us, trying to make us spin, "from the extreme hazard on."

John is bailing like crazy, but there's no slowing this boat down here. Ahead of me the big rock wall looms, blunt, impassive, all the water I'm riding thundering into it and churning and surging at its base. I find the surprising strength of adrenaline and pull off the rock wall without so much as kissing it. Kris loses her balance in one of the after-waves and tumbles into the relatively calm water. "Save the Book!" John yells before pulling her back in. This is what I love about the Middle Fork. Only 282 rapids to go.

It's late in the day and we're all exhausted. There's only a few class I and II rapids between us and the campsite I'm headed for at Sheepeater Hot Springs.

We camp above the springs, leaving the main campsite for a bigger commercial group. I start dinner—halibut steaks, baked with scallions and tomatoes in the Dutch oven, corn on the cob, and fresh asparagus—while John and Kris go to check out the hot pool. I know I will get my chance, when the lazy June dark finally comes, and there's a bite to the air, and I can have the pool all to myself and watch the stars dive toward me out of the Milky Way.

When I open my eyes the next morning five inches of snow weigh down the top of the tent. I put coffee and hot cereal on the Coleman stove, but everyone's more interested in making a beeline for the hot springs. It is June 21, I realize, the longest day of the year, the first day of summer, everywhere but here on the Middle Fork, where the weather gods sometimes get confused.

In a little while we'll have to make a decision: whether to sit in a hot pool all day watching the snow fall out of the spruce trees, or break camp and get in the boat and get a lot of cold water splashed in our faces. I know the vote will be in favor of a layover day, in spite of the fact that we are only twelve miles into a ninety-seven-mile trip, in spite of our real-life commitments that an extra day on the river might make difficult to meet.

Today we will sit back, breathe the too-cold mountain air, and hope the sun comes out tomorrow. Tomorrow, before lunchtime, we'll hit Pistol Creek Rapid, a crazy kind of a k-turn in the river that at this level may need more strength than I have to get past all the boulders and keep us right side up. And as the current above Pistol grabs our boat and I'm pulling for all I'm worth away from the huge suckhole Kris is reading about, I'll remember, just for an instant, the other reason I love the Middle Fork: it lets me walk that fragile shimmery line between all that's brave and all that's crazy, the same line I was walking when I made the west my home.

On (Not) Climbing
the Grand Teton

They rise out of the Snake River Valley like a rich dark promise. Taller than the Grand Canyon is deep, sharper than the blade of a bread knife, the Tetons stand more than seven thousand feet above the town of Jackson Hole, Wyoming. And though there are many formidable peaks in the Teton Range, there is no mistaking the Grand Teton, 13,770 feet above sea level, steely gray, deeply fissured, and bent slightly southward, as if after surviving the cataclysm that must have made it, it wanted to rest awhile, and turn its face to the sun.

"The Grand," as it is known to all who have had the pleasure to live under it, or ski beside it, or hike around it, or climb to the top of it, is more than the highest mountain in what many would call the continental United States' most spectacular range. It is a magnet, a motherlode, a home base to a breed of people who have no home. Not just people who ski and climb, but *skiers* and *climbers*, the ones who relegate real-life activities like laundry and relationships to those couple of weeks in the spring and fall when the lifts have closed but it's too slick to climb, or the snow has come but the runs aren't yet open.

The Grand calls out to those people, calls them from their lives in Wisconsin or Florida, calls them from their high-paying jobs and their reasonably happy marriages, and says, "Come see what its like to ski Corbett's when the snow's still soft, come see what it's like to have your morning coffee after fourteen pitches up the Exum Route to the top of the Grand."

There was a time in my life when I was one of those people. When the rivers and the mountains spoke to me and I took on any challenge they offered, however ill-suited I might have been to the task. Now I have learned to be a little more selective about which challenges I accept. I know the mediums in which my body performs best and they are the soft ones: water, snow, the back of a particularly responsive horse; and the ones in which my body stumbles: rock, pavement, and anywhere more than twenty feet off the ground.

Imagine my surprise, then, when I found myself dangling by a 150-foot length of rope on a rock face called the Open Book several thousand feet below the summit of the Grand Teton with Dick Dorworth—the fastest man on skis in 1963—holding fast to the other end.

But there I was.

Dick Dorworth is one of the guides in the world-renowned Exum Mountaineering School, a school where a first-time climber can take an intensive three-day course in mountaineering and, if the guide judges her capable, spend the next two days climbing the Grand.

Perhaps what went wrong in my case is that we tried to do

the whole three days of training in one day. Or perhaps, as Dick said, I just didn't really want to climb that mountain.

But on the morning of my training session, I thought I did. It was late September, the air as clear and fine and sharp as the big mountain that loomed above us. We passed a cow moose on the way to the practice area near Hidden Falls, and I took it as a good omen. It was early when we started, and the trail was trafficked with big slow birds Dick didn't know the name of—ruffed grouse, I found out later, they were called.

In spite of all my rock-related, height-related fears, I was excited about the climbing. Dick was both patient and supportive and I cruised through what would have been the first day's training climbs easily before we sat down for lunch in the shade of a huge overhanging wall.

When he motioned to the perfectly vertical rock face that adjoined the overhang and said, "That's what we climb after lunch," I was sure he was only kidding. "And if you make it, then we cap the day off with this—" he pointed directly overhead—"the advanced rappel."

After one short morning Dick knew me well enough to know this was the right incentive. Though I'd only done it a few times, I loved rappelling, loved the trust I had to put in the equipment, loved the moment of stepping over the edge, the last contact with the rock before it curved away in an overhang. I loved hanging there, free, for a moment, the rope in my hands controlling my descent, and I loved looking out over all that surrounded me, which in this case would be the sparkling surface of Jackson Lake and the clouds making shadows across the Teton valley floor.

I got off to a pretty good start, despite the Open Book's

daunting height and sheerness, surprising myself by climbing the first seventy-five feet or so without so much as a hesitation. Then I looked down.

My knees started doing the sewing machine thing, and I felt fatigue in my joints from the morning. There was a lot more rock above than below me, I noticed, and to continue I would have to move laterally, toward the crease in the "book," and use a hand jam, a technique whose logic my stubborn brain would not quite let me believe.

As any climber will tell you, one moment of faithlessness leads in a straight plumb line to another. The hand jam wouldn't work, the toehold was much too small, even the place where I'd been resting, which just moments ago seemed so secure, was suddenly fraught with unspeakable danger. The only thing left to do was fling myself upward, sideways, and pray that by some miracle I stuck to the rock.

I didn't. Stick, that is. I fell, ten feet or so and clunked hard with my head and my knees and my elbows into the rock, every ounce of my weight hanging from my harness and Dick well above me, and I couldn't get a hand- or a toehold to save my life.

"Stand on your feet, Pam," came Dick's voice from above, and I looked down again, at the sixty-five feet of wall below me, to the ground that I would kneel down and kiss if only I could get to it, and I said to myself, "Goddammit, Pam, how did you get here again?"

"Climb this rock, Pam," Dick said. "Now."

And I tried to do just that. And I had faith in my equipment, and more faith still in Dick. And my head knew this was only a practice run, for heaven's sake, the bunny hill of climbing, and that if I needed to I could try again and even fail again, I could hang from that rock all day without getting seriously hurt. But somewhere between my head and the rest of my body I missed a connection, and my heart pounded as hard as if I was already cut loose and falling, and my arms and my legs started shaking worse than ever, and I clawed and clawed at the wall like a bug on the inside of a water glass, with no result at all.

"Stand on your feet, Pam." Came the voice, calm, a little bored even. *You didn't know the name of that bird this morning*, I thought in a completely uncalled-for moment of vindictiveness. *You didn't even know the moose we saw was a cow.*

"Hey Dick," I ventured. "What would you think about letting me down?"

"I can't do that, Pam," he said.

"Is it that you *can't* put me down, Dick," I said, "or that you *won't?*"

"Oh, I *can* put you down," he said. "But if I do, then you can't do the rappel."

"That may be true according to the laws in your universe," I said. "In my universe I can hike around the back side of this rock and do the rappel anyway."

"We all need challenges in our lives, Pam," he said, and I thought about the top three items on my current list of challenges: a chronically unfinished novel, an impossible relationship with a difficult man, a close friend—an angel of a man, really—dying of advanced melanoma. I needed to climb the bunny slope of Exum Mountaineering School like I needed a hole in the head, but I was mad now. I dug my fingernails into the rock and started climbing.

I'm not sure what happened in the next minute or two. I imagine there was a lot of cursing, several ungraceful postures, and judging by the minor abrasions I discovered on nearly every exposed piece of my body when I got to the top, a little pain, though I didn't feel it at the time.

"There," Dick said. "Now doesn't that feel a lot better?"

But I was shaking too much to tell.

"Okay," Dick said, "one more pitch and we'll call it a day." I looked up at the rock rising another hundred feet above the ledge we sat on.

"Dick," I said, "I think we both agree that whether or not I make it the rest of the way up this rock, I'm not going to be Grand Teton material."

"I'm afraid that's true," he said.

"I don't know if you will understand this," I said, "but in my life right now, the bigger challenge is to say I'm scared, I don't like this, and I want to go down."

Dick studied my face for a moment, then the rope in his hand. "Okay," he said, and I thought that would be all, but then he said, "Is there anything I could do to make the day better?"

"Yeah," I said, smiling. "You could let me do the advanced rappel."

And he did.

And it was wonderful. But I went home sad and disconsolate anyway. The Rocky Mountains have been, since I have been old enough to think clearly, my church and my religion, and to fail in them, in whatever small or specific way, felt much too much like a failure of my soul. I needed to create another challenge, something that let me be in the mountains the way I wanted to be there, with my hands free enough to take pictures and touch tree bark, and my head free enough to take it all in.

If I couldn't get to the top of the Grand Teton, I decided, I'd learn what I could from hiking in its shadow. With the shortening September days and the unpredictable weather, a day hike of twenty miles and an elevation gain of four thousand feet—up Cascade Canyon and over Paintbrush Divide— would be just challenge enough.

I was up at first light, and it was well below freezing. I tried to ignore the signs at the trailhead about grizzly bear attacks and violent rutting moose in Paintbrush Canyon, about how I should avoid hiking alone or during the low-light, high-predation hours between dusk and dawn.

By the time I had climbed my first five hundred feet into Cascade Canyon the air was softening and I was shedding layers like crazy. The morning fog had lifted and the ground smelled leafy and loamy in the sunshine, like it was done with summer, and waiting for the snow. Cascade Canyon was flat and broad and I shared the trail with more deer than I could keep track of. Every now and then the Grand, awash in morning sun, winked out at me from above the canyon wall.

On the way to Lake Solitude the trail rose above tree line, and behind me the walls of the canyon formed a soft cradle of reds and browns and yellows that held the peak of the Grand perfectly inside it, and I could see every block and fissure, every snowfield, every steep pitch I wouldn't be climbing, backlit and magnificent against a perfect blue sky.

I put my foot in Lake Solitude's icy water. I put my hands

on every rock I went by. I played with my camera, shooting patterns I saw in the surface of boulders, the occasional shock of red in the mostly brown tundra, the emerald-green siltiness of the high and tiny Mica Lake. And I shot the Grand again and again as it rose higher still out of its cradle, as its shadows lengthened and shifted as the sun tumbled over it. I reached the top of the spectacular 10,700-foot Paintbrush Divide, still three thousand feet below the Grand's summit, sufficiently reverent, sufficiently awed.

It was four o'clock, and I had four thousand feet and a lot of miles to make before nightfall. I started down the much steeper Paintbrush Canyon, making time like crazy, hoofing it down the trail at top speed, my strong legs pumping, my pack feeling light as a feather, feeling the faith of an outdoors-woman again. I was certain I was going to make it back to the truck within the envelope of visible light, when I heard a noise that made me stop dead in my tracks.

It was a huff, but *loud*, the unmistakable sound of an ani-mal—a big animal—exhaling, a noise they make when they are threatened, or when they are mating, or in the moment just before they attack. I waited five long seconds before I heard the huff again, no louder, but this time I could pinpoint its direction. Whatever it was, it was in a stand of ponderosa pine not five feet from where I'd just passed on the trail. Whatever it was, it could smell me, and so far it wasn't show-ing any signs of being scared.

The musk of something huge and dark hung like a cloud in the clean evening air. I grabbed my camera from my pack and cut a wide swath around the ponderosas on my way to a glacial boulder I hoped I could climb. The rock was steep-sided and smooth as glass but I dug my toes and fingers in just like I'd practiced and made it easily to the top.

"Thanks, Dick," I said out loud, laughing, but was silenced by another huff, this one louder, a little angrier than before.

From the top of the rock I could see that my companion was a big bull moose, the biggest I'd seen this side of Alaska, and I could see the paddles of his antlers, broad and blond and almost glowing in the twilight as he thumped them again and again against the thick trunk of the tree. His dark head, his huge improbable nose, was just a suggestion in the shadows, but I thought I could make out one dark eye gleaming.

Maybe he was mad because I'd invaded his territory, or maybe it was time for his yearly drop, or maybe there was a lady other than me in the vicinity he was trying to impress. But he wasn't getting anywhere for all his passionate thumping, and I thought of myself scrabbling up there on the Open Book, all the will and rage and desire I'm capable of pumping through my body, and all of it to no avail.

"I know how you feel," I said, softly, but the moose had forgotten all about me.

Until my film rewound, that is, and the camera made a noise he'd never heard before, and he huffed again and made four steps of a mock charge towards me.

"Easy, big boy," I said, and he pawed the ground and fixed me with that gleaming eye, and I slid down the back side of the rock, grabbed my pack, and hit the trail running. I could hear him coming behind me, the heavy footfalls, not running but walking steadily, the huffing softer now, but regular, in time with his step.

He followed me as far as the next set of switchbacks, but

always at a respectful distance, a little like a gentleman not sure if he wants to make a pass. When I looked back the last time he was nothing more than a dark shape against a darkening sky, but I could tell by the way he held his head that he hadn't taken his eye off me, and he wouldn't until he knew I was gone for good.

It was well past dark when I got back to the trailhead, but the harvest moon was bright and full and I had no trouble finding my way. The woods were full of the rumbling of animals, and I could hear the elk bugling their unearthly music in the meadows, a song so full of longing it silenced even the crickets and the owls. Above it all the summit of the Grand rose to bathe itself in the moonlight: stony and radiant, as good as a million miles away.

A few
good
men

―――――――――

In the Company
of Fishermen

I can't remember the last time I envied a man, or, in fact, if I ever have. I have loved men, hated them, befriended them, taken care of them, and all too often compromised my sense of self for them, but I don't think I have ever looked at a man and actually coveted something his maleness gave him. And yet envy was at least one of the surprising things I felt last spring when I found myself standing armpit-deep in a freshwater stream at 2:00 a.m., near Interlochen, Michigan, fly-casting for steelhead with a bunch of male poets.

Winters are long in northern Michigan, and dark and frozen. Spring is late and wet and full of spirit-breaking storms. The landscape is primarily forest and water and has not been tamed like most of the midwest. Both the wildness and the hardship show on the faces of the people who choose to live there.

When a man named Jack Driscoll first calls and invites me to Interlochen, he tells me about the Academy, a place where talented high school students from forty-one states and fifteen countries are given a lot of time to develop their art. Although he makes it clear that I will be expected to read from my fiction and talk to the students about craft, every other time we speak on the phone, all he really wants to talk about is fishing.

For all the time I spend outdoors, I am not much of a fisherman. And fly-fishing, like all religions, is something I respect but don't particularly understand. If Jack bothers to ask me if I want to go fishing, I will say yes. I have always said yes, and as a result the shape of my life has been a long series of man-inspired adventures, and I have gone tripping along behind those men, full of strength and will and only a half-baked kind of competence, my goal being not to excel, but to simply keep up with them, to not become a problem, to be a good sport. It is a childhood thing (I was my father's only son), and I laugh at all the places this particular insecurity has taken me: sheep hunting in Alaska, helicopter skiing in Montana, cliff diving in the Bahamas, ice climbing in the Yukon territory. Mostly I have outgrown the need to impress men in this fashion; in the adventures I take these days, I make the rules. But, as my trip to Michigan draws nearer, I feel a familiar and demented excitement to be back at the mercy of a bunch of lunatic outdoorsmen, a stubborn novice with something older than time to prove.

I fly up to Traverse City on what the woman at the United Express counter calls the "big" plane, a twin-engine that bumps between thunderstorms and patches of dense fog for an hour before skidding to a stop on a bleak and rainy runway surrounded by leafless April woods.

I am greeted by what looks like a small committee of fit and weathered middle-aged men. Their names are Jack Driscoll, Mike Delp, Nick Bozanic, and Doug Stanton. Their books are titled after the landscape that dominates their lives, collections of poetry called *Under the Influence of Water*, *The Long Drive Home*, and *Over the Graves of Horses*, and Jack's award-winning collection of stories, *Wanting Only to Be Heard*. They fight over my luggage, hand me snacks and sodas and beers, and all but carry me to the car on the wave of their enthusiasm.

"Weather's been good," Mike says, by way of a greeting. "The lake ice is breaking."

"It's a real late run for the steelhead," Doug says. "You're just in time."

"Any minute now, any minute now," Jack says, his mind full of the long dark bodies of fish in the river, and then, "You've got a reading in forty-five minutes, then a dinner that should be over by ten. The president of the local community college wants to meet you. At midnight, we fish."

By 12:25 a.m. I am dressed in my long underwear, Jack's camouflage sweat clothes, Mike's neoprene liners, Doug's waders, and Nick's hat. I look like the Michelin tire man, the waders so big and stiff I can barely put one foot in front of the other. We pile into Mike's Montero, rods and reels jangling in the back. Jack and Mike and Doug and I. Nick, each man has told me (privately, in a quiet, apprehensive voice), is recovering from bursitis and a divorce, and for one or another of those reasons, he will not fish this year.

No one asks me if I'm tired, nor do I ask them. These men have had nine months of winter to catch up on their sleep, cabin fever reflecting in their eyes like exclamations. The steelhead will start running soon, maybe tonight, and there is no question about where they should be.

It takes almost an hour to get to the river with what I quickly understand is an obligatory stop at the Sunoco in the tiny town of Honor for day-old doughnuts and Coca-Cola and banter with the cashier. Along the way we listen to what Mike and Jack say is their latest road tape, three Greg Brown songs recorded over and over to fill a ninety-minute drive. "Gonna meet you after midnight," say the lyrics repeatedly, "at the Dream Café."

The rotating sign on the Honor State Bank says 1:51 a.m. and twenty-two degrees. The men have bet on what the temperature will be. They have also bet on how many cars we will pass on the two-lane highway, how many deer we will see in the woods between Mike's house and the bridge, if it will snow or rain, and, if so, how hard (hardness gauged by comparison with other nights' fishing). Doug wins the temperature bet, closest without going over, at twenty-one degrees.

The betting is all part of a long conversational rap among them, a rap that moves from Mike's last fish to Jack's latest fiction to concern for Nick and his lost house to the girl at the Sunoco to an in-unison sing-along to their favorite Greg Brown lyrics. The whole conversation is less like speaking really and more like singing, a song they've spent years and years of these cold spring nights together learning, nights anybody anywhere else in the world would call winter, nights filled with an expectation that can only be called boyish and shadowed by too much of the grown-up knowledge that can ultimately defeat men.

Sometimes they remember I am there; sometimes they forget I am a woman.

I feel, in those moments, like I've gone undercover, like I've been granted security clearance to a rare and private work of art. And though I have always believed that women bond faster, tighter, deeper than men could ever dream of, there is something simple and pure between these men, a connection so thick and dense and timeless that I am fascinated, and jealous, and humbled, all at the same time.

"Shit," Jack says. "Look at 'em all." We have come finally out of the woods and to a bridge no longer than the width of the two-lane roadway. As impossible as it is for me to believe, at 2:00 a.m. the gravel areas on both sides of the bridge are lined with pickups, a counterculture of night stalkers, two and three trucks deep.

I can see by the posture of the men who line the bridge and look gloomily over the edge that they do not teach poetry at Interlochen Arts Academy. One of them staggers toward the truck, reeling drunk. A boy of nine or ten, dressed all in camouflage, tries to steady him from behind.

"They ain't here yet," the old man says, an edge in his voice like desperation. "It may be they just ain't coming."

"They'll be here," Jack says, easing himself out of the Montero and steering the man away from the broken piece of bridge railing. "It's been a long winter for everybody," Jack says, almost cooing, and the old man drunkenly, solemnly nods.

Mike pulls me out of the truck and hands me a flashlight. We creep to the edge of the bridge and peer over. "Just on for a second and off," he whispers. Even to me it is unmistakable; the flashlight illuminates a long, dark shape already half under the pylon. "Don't say anything," Mike mouths to me soundlessly. Jack leaves the old-timer to sleep in his car and joins us. Mike holds up one finger and Jack nods. "We'll go downstream," Jack says after some consideration. "Nobody's gonna do any good here."

We drive downriver while Mike points out all the sights as if we can see them—a place called the Toilet Hole, where Doug and Nick got lucky, the place Mike got his car stuck so bad four-wheel drive couldn't help him, the place Jack caught last year's biggest fish. We can see the headlights of people who are smelt-dipping out where the river empties into the lake, and a red-and-white channel marker lit up and looming in the darkness, its base still caked with lake ice and snow.

We drop Doug off at his favorite hole near the mouth of the river, drive back upstream a few hundred yards, park the Montero, and step out into the night.

"It's a little bit of a walk from here," Mike says, "and the mud's pretty deep." It is impossible for me to imagine how I will move my stiff and padded legs through deep mud, how, at twenty-two degrees, I will step into that swift and icy river, much less stand in it for a couple of hours. I can't imagine how, with all these clothes and pitch dark around me, I'll be able to cast my fly with anything resembling grace.

Two steps away from the truck and already I feel the suction. The mud we are walking in ranges from mid-calf to mid-thigh deep. I'm following Jack like a puppy, trying to walk where he walks, step where he steps. I get warm with the effort, and a little careless, and suddenly there's nothing beneath me and I'm in watery mud up to my waist. Mike and Jack, each on one arm, pull me out so fast it seems like part of the choreography.

"Let's try to cross the river," says Jack, and before I can even brace for the cold, we are in it, thigh . . . hip . . . waist deep, and I feel the rush of the current tug me toward Lake Michigan. "One foot in front of the other," Jack says. "The hole's right in front of you; when you're ready, go ahead and cast."

I lift the rod uneasily into the night, close my eyes and try to remember how they did it in *A River Runs Through It*, and then bring it down too fast and too hard with an ungraceful splat. "Let out a little more line," Jack says, so gently it's like he's talking to himself. A few more splats, a little more line, and I am making casts that aren't embarrassing. Jack moves without speaking to help Mike with a snarl in his line. "This is your night, Delp," Jack says, his shadowy form floating away from me, a dark and legless ghost.

What in the world are you doing here? a voice giggles up from inside me, and the answers sweep past me, too fast to catch: because I can't turn down a challenge, because my father wanted a boy, because touching this wildness is the best way I know to undermine sadness, because of the thin shimmery line I am seeing between the dark river and the even darker sky.

Soon I stop thinking about being washed to Lake Michigan. I marvel at how warm I am in the waders, so warm and buoyant that I forget myself from time to time and dip some unprotected part of me, my hand or my elbow, into the icy water. A deer crackles sticks in the forest across the river; an angry beaver slaps his tail. In whispers we take turns identifying Ursa Major, Draco, Cassiopeia, Mars, and Jupiter and murmur at the infrequent but lovely falling stars.

When we are quiet I can hear a faint crashing—constant, reverberant—sounding in the dark for all the world like the heartbeat of the earth. "Lake Michigan coming over the breakwater," Jack says to my unasked question. "There must be a big wind on the other side."

My fishing is steadily improving: every fifth or seventh cast hangs a long time in the air and falls lightly, almost without sound.

"You know," Jack says, "there aren't too many people who could come out here like this and not hook themselves or me or the shoreline . . . isn't that right, Delp?" Mike murmurs in agreement, and my head swells with ridiculously disproportionate pride.

The constellations disappear, and a light snow begins falling. "God, I love the weather," Mike says, his voice a mixture of sarcasm and sincerity, and for a while there is only the whisper of the line and the flies.

"Fish!" Jack shouts suddenly. "Fish on the line!" I am startled almost out of my footing, as if I've forgotten what we've come here for, as if the silence of the night and the rhythm of the flies hitting the water have become reason enough. We reel in our lines and watch Jack land his fish. It is long and thin and its speckled belly gleams silver as it thrashes in the tiny beam of the flashlight. Jack looks at us helplessly, delighted by his luck and yet wishing, simultaneously, that it had been me who caught the fish, wishing even harder, I can see, that it had been Mike.

We fish a little longer, but now there's no need to stay. The spell has been broken; the first steelhead has been caught in its journey up the Platte.

"Let's wade downriver a little," Jack says, when we've reeled in our lines, "to try to avoid the mud." I take short rapid breaths as we move through the water. "This part is deep," Jack says. "Take it slow."

The water creeps up my chest and into my armpits; I'm walking, weightless, through a dark and watery dream. For a moment there is nothing but my forward momentum and the lift of water under the soles of my boots that keep me from going under. Then I feel the bank rise suddenly beneath my feet.

"No problem," I say, just before my foot slips and I do go under, head and all, into the icy current. I thrash my arms toward shore, and Jack grabs me. "Better get you home," he says, as the cold I've ignored for hours moves through my body with logarithmic speed. "You've gotta meet students in a couple of hours." Back at the truck Doug is curled under a blanket like a dog.

The next day Jack sleeps while Mike makes sure I meet my classes. The students are bright, skeptical, interested. My head buzzes with the heat of the all-nighter, a darkness, like the river dark, threatening to close in. Mike and I drink bad machine coffee in one of the tunnels that connect the English department to the other school buildings, tunnels to keep the students from getting lost in the storms that bring the blowing snow.

"It's hard to explain how much I love these guys," Mike says suddenly, as if I've asked him. "I don't know what I'd do without what we have."

The cement walls of this poor excuse for a lounge move in on us like the weather, and this poet who more resembles a wrestler looks for a moment as if he might cry.

It is late in the evening. I have met three classes, talked to at least thirty students, given another reading, signed books in Traverse City, and as part of an orgy of a potluck, cooked elk steaks, rare, on the grill. Mike, in his other favorite role of DJ, plays one moody song after another on the stereo: John Prine, John Gorka, and early Bonnie Raitt. We are all a little high from the good food and tequila. Mike's ten-year-old daughter Jamie and Jack dance cheek to cheek in their socks on the living-room floor.

"So are we gonna do it?" Jack says when the song ends, a sparkle in his eye that says the river is always in him, whether he's standing in it or not. This fish-and-fiction marathon is in its thirty-eighth hour, and I have moved beyond tired now to some new level of consciousness.

I have spent too much of my life proving I can be one of the guys, never saying uncle, never admitting I'm tired, or hurting, or cold. Tonight I am all three, but the thing that makes me nod my head and say *yes I want to go back again and stand in that icy river* has nothing, for a change, to do with my father, or my childhood, or all the things in the world I need to prove. It is the potent and honest feeling between these men that I covet, that I can't miss an opportunity to be close to. I have stumbled, somehow, onto this rare pack of animals who know I am there and have decided, anyway, to let me watch them at their dance. I want to memorize their movements. I want to take these river nights home with me for the times when the darkness is even heavier than it is in this Michigan sky.

A flurry of rubber and neoprene, and we're back inside the Montero. Greg Brown is singing the song about the laughing river. "This is your night, Delp," Jack says. "I can feel it." Around the next bend will be Honor's scattered lights.

I Was a Captain in
Colonel Bob's Army

I have been a lot of places in my life, some of the world's most secret hideouts, expanses of ocean, desert, or mountaintop on which I felt I was among the first to lay eyes. I loved every destination—to a greater or lesser degree—not only for its charms and character, but also for its newness to me. This year I embarked on a journey to a place darker, more remote, certainly more mysterious and a hundred times more frightening than the jungles of Africa, more isolated than the valleys of the Himalaya. With the help of a process called EMDR and the guidance of a wonderful therapist, I entered the forbidden country of my childhood memories, a place locked behind a wall more formidable than any I had seen in my travels, a place I wouldn't and couldn't ever go to before, a place I went to more than forty foreign countries to avoid.

As with any trip, things did not go exactly as I expected. Nothing looked like I had imagined it would, I had brought all the wrong things with me, and what I had thought would be the high points turned out to be the lows. In time I will find a way to write about those low points, the terror and the violence that kept me from visiting this country, kept the voices of my childhood silent for so long. But like all adventures, this one was also full of blessings. Unexpected angels, who had gotten locked up with all the trauma, showed up, like they always do, right when I wanted to call the whole trip off and go home.

They say that children who have grown up with rage and chaos and who still manage to survive into middle age as functioning and somewhat hopeful adults have—in almost every case—found a counterexample to their parents, someone who was reliable and steady, who served as a reality check for kids whose home life made it impossible to tell the difference between right and wrong.

I had three angels that I know of for sure, though there are more back there, still hiding. The first was a baby-sitter named Martha Washington, a tough old ex–supply sergeant in the U.S. Army who taught me how to read when I was only two, paid me a quarter every time I jumped off the high dive, and always let me have whatever I wanted for dinner. She did much more than that: she gave me the only unconditional love I got in those days, and stole me several times from my parents when they were deep in their alcoholic fury, threatening not to give me back if they didn't change their ways. We moved away from her when I was five, right after my broken femur had healed enough so I could escape to her house on my tricycle.

There was a teacher named Mr. Kashner who switched from fifth to sixth grade the same year I did. He made me believe in my brains, and how I might use them to get out of trouble and away from my family. He didn't mind if I broke the rules as long as I was being creative, and he made me feel worthwhile in a way I had never felt before.

But this essay is about the most unlikely angel, a gruff, more-than-middle-aged man named Colonel Bob Miller who saved not only me, but all the other neighborhood kids from whatever bad things went on in their homes. One weekend a summer, for no other reason than because he liked to, Colonel Bob Miller took all the kids from my Bethlehem, Pennsylvania, neighborhood to a place called Apache Gulch.

Imagine twenty-five children, ages five to fifteen, all lined up with their slumber-party sleeping bags and their plastic ponchos, leaning on boxes of baked beans and marshmallows and hot dog buns, on cases of beer and soda, on Army-issue cots and hatchets and flashlights. We all lined up according to rank, because we were all members of Colonel Bob's army, where you started as a buck private, but if you did what you were told, if you passed the Bravery Test without chickening out or crying, if you sat out your night watch without waking a grown-up, if you hauled the grown-ups' beer without complaint, if you took your turn cooking and cleaning, if you were generally speaking a good kid, you would, the next afternoon, be promoted to corporal, and then sergeant, and so on, up through all the ranks of every branch of the armed services, warrant officers first, second, third, and fourth class, and junior and senior chief petty officers. And it didn't matter how many years you went on Colonel Bob's weekends, or how many ranks you went through; there were no generals in this army, and the only colonel was Bob.

Bob, of course, wasn't really a colonel. I remember hearing once that he was a captain, or a corporal, which shows how much I know about the military, but whatever he was in real life didn't matter; he was Colonel Bob to us.

After much arguing about who would ride in which station wagon, and hugs and goodbyes from those parents who saw fit to come see their children off, we loaded the cars for the trip "out west." One by one we piled under the wool blankets, made hotter and scratchier by the Pennsylvania heat. It was far and away the most miserable part of the weekend, but if we came out from under those blankets to peek or sneeze, or even just for a breath of the relatively cool station-wagon air, we would be demoted before the trip even got under way. Besides, we'd been told that the Indians out west didn't like children, that they might take it upon themselves to turn one of us into an afternoon snack, so under the blankets we stayed.

"We just crossed the Mississippi!" Colonel Bob called out from the driver's seat, and sometime later, "There goes the wide Missourra!" Later still, when we thought we really might pass out from the heat and motion and the lack of oxygen, the car screeched to a halt.

"Ugguh, ugguh, whoa!" a voice said.

"Noosho, ugguh, Noa!" Colonel Bob's voice came back. Because for most of us, this was our third or sixth or twelfth time under the blanket, we knew we had reached the edge of Indian Country, and Colonel Bob was getting permission from the big chief, asking him to let us into Apache Gulch.

The car crawled forward, more slowly now.

"Look at that!" It was the voice of Bob Lilienthal, Colonel Bob's right-hand man on every trip. "I believe that's a dead Indian floating down the river."

We squirmed under our blankets, but no one looked up.

We knew the cars would stop soon and we'd tumble out, maybe in time to get a glimpse of the dead Indian. But he had always floated downriver by the time we got free.

The River, as we called it, was little more than a creek; our campsite, which Colonel Bob called Dismal Swamp, was just that. Turning a swamp into a campsite took a lot of work, but that's what Colonel Bob knew was good for us and we did it, the worst jobs going to those with the lowest ranks, while the high-ranking officers—mostly adult friends of Bob's—lay on their cots sipping beer and delegating.

We all wore armbands—I know how that sounds, but we did, with our rank emblazoned upon them. The rules were that you could ask anyone lower in rank than you to do anything, but you were required to do anything that a higher-ranking camper asked of you. While it wasn't a very democratic system, it certainly was efficient, and we turned a swamp into a livable campsite in no time flat.

When camp was set up, with its separate officers and troop quarters, a kitchen, a blazing fire, and a gallows (in case any-one acted so badly they'd have to be court-martialed and then hanged), we went on a hike. Colonel Bob taught the new kids how to read a compass, and relied on those of us who knew how to find the way.

Dinner was as predictable as the Girl Scouts (an organiza-tion I never joined, quitting Brownies after only one day): beans and franks, s'mores and "bug juice," with extra beans for everyone.

We lingered over dinner, all of us excited and afraid of what would come after dark: the Bravery Test, the single most important criterion for advancement in rank. Some years we had to walk with nothing in our hands, following flashlights that were hanging from trees; other times we carried our own flashlights and followed white markers in the trees. In every case we were alone in the woods, in the dark, and it was scary.

We sat on our bunks waiting to be called to the campfire for our debriefing from Colonel Bob. When he said my name it was serious and quiet, and I walked over to the fire and took a seat next to him. He wanted to make sure I knew how to use my compass; he wanted to make sure I felt confident alone in the woods. He wanted to make sure I knew exactly what would be required of me. I would begin just to the north of camp and look for white markers hanging in the trees. I was allowed to take my flashlight and my Swiss army knife. I was never to walk away from one marker until I had the next one in sight. If I didn't follow those directions and got myself into a position where I couldn't see any markers, either in front or behind, I was to sit down right where I was and not make a sound and wait for the Bravery Test to be over. When I had passed twenty-seven markers there would be a compass hanging on a tree. I was to take a reading of 120 degrees and walk for one hundred paces. Did I have any questions? Was I scared? Well, I was right to be. The woods were a serious place that demanded my utmost concentration.

I remember these as some of the best and most intensely honest moments of my childhood: someone taking me seriously enough to try to teach me something real, the adrenaline racing through me, the chance to make someone I cared about proud. A final check to make sure my compass was working, and I was off.

There were always noises in the woods: *Deer?* I wondered.

Bear? Or was it the grown-ups hidden off to the side of the trail, waiting in case one of us fell or panicked or got off the track? It seemed like grounds for demotion even to hope for that kind of security. There were lights on the hillside above us and shouts that sounded for all the world like war whoops: Indians, maybe, planning a war party, or deciding which child to eat for dinner.

I counted off the white markers, careful not to lose sight of the one I was walking toward, but checking back every ten steps to make sure I could see the one behind. I lost count after twenty and finally saw the compass hanging in the tree. I took a reading, took ten of the hundred prescribed paces, felt a big bear paw on my shoulder and heard the voice of Bob Lilienthal. *Sit down. Congratulations. You passed.* I sat perfectly still while one flashlight at a time moved towards me through the woods. When everybody was finished, we made our way back the mile or so to camp.

Some years not everybody made it. Some years we got back to camp missing a kid and a search party was formed and we all worked together in that, too. I don't know if Colonel Bob had kids get lost on purpose just so we could find them, or if they actually did, but it was always the older ones who didn't turn up, kids who ought to have had an easy time of the Bravery Test, kids who maybe were so old they didn't mind getting court-martialed, dropped a few ranks while the rest of us stepped ahead.

After the Bravery Test, the night watches began: one hour, two people, three marshmallows, and one hot dog. If an Indian came into camp, we were to wake up one grown-up, if a bear came in, another; if an Indian and a bear came at the

same time, we were to wake up Bob Lilienthal. Under no cir-
cumstances were we to wake up Colonel Bob; he told us he
needed his sleep. But he was roaming around the woods half
the night anyway, setting off single firecrackers a hundred
yards from camp and making big stomping noises in the
woods. We huddled up next to our watch partners, even if we
didn't like them, split the hot dog and the third marshmallow,
tried our best to stay awake.

Falling asleep on night watch was the *second* most reprehen-
sible thing you could do after flunking the Bravery Test, and it
guaranteed not a court-martial but a demotion. There was
always the chance that you would be asked to testify for or
against your watch partner during the promotion and demotion ceremonies. I was an expert at staying up all night, a trait
that served me well in my unpredictable household. I always
volunteered for the dead man's watch, 3:30–4:30 a.m., because I
knew it gave me extra points with the Colonel, and also because
most of the fireworks and foot stomping had stopped by then.

In the morning it was Sunday, and Colonel Bob turned into
Reverend Bob and we had church around the burned-out
campfire. It was simple and beautiful. My personal religion
comes mostly from those fireside talks. Bob would talk about
how lucky we were to have the woods, how lucky we were to
be out in them together. Then he would ask us each to say
something we loved about the outdoors. Then it was time for
the war games.

Girls on one boundary of the forest, boys on the other. Bob's
grown daughter coached the girls' team, his son-in-law
coached the boys, and they always went home not speaking.
The object of the game: to get across the playing field (several

hundred yards of forest) without being spotted and called
Out, to call the boys Out when you see them, to get more girls
across the line than boys. Loser buys ice cream the night after
we get home.

All that remained after the war games were the promotions
and demotions, a striking of camp that most of my grown-up
environmentalist friends would approve of, and a long, hot,
and exhausted under-the-blanket ride from Apache Gulch
back home.

Apache Gulch, I now know, had another name: Monocacy
Park, City of Bethlehem. Wilder than a real city park because
Bethlehem wasn't a real city, the park filled the small canyon
that Monocacy Creek cut alongside the town. The distance we
rode under those blankets each summer, for what felt like
hours in the sweltering heat, was exactly seven miles.

In the process of recovering memories, there are more than
a few surprises, but none more pleasantly startling than this:
to remember these weekends preserved like gems in their
entirety, and then to realize "going out west" only meant the
west side of town.

To get from Colonel Bob's house to Apache Gulch we would
have driven through the suburb where we lived, past the shopping mall where five years later I would get arrested for
shoplifting a cat candle, past the Exxon station where ten years
later a high school classmate would be blown to smithereens in
a gasoline explosion, past the ice-skating rink where I would
learn to skate forwards and backwards and eventually learn
how to kiss. It was the skating rink, lit up at night and noisy,
that had become the Indian campfire in our minds.

There were soccer fields in Monocacy Park, bike paths, a

jogging track, but there was also a several-acre area left wild and overgrown, and somehow Colonel Bob kept us close enough inside its borders that we were able to believe we were in a place as wild as his imagination. We were able to believe, if only for a weekend, we were really out west.

I think about that now, about the power of imagination, about Santa Claus and the tooth fairy, about what belief is to a child who is afraid all the time. I was a smart kid, way too smart for my age, and when I look back I ask myself how old I would have been when I asked the inevitable questions. If we're out west, then why is it still Saturday, why didn't we ever stop for gas, why can't we ride with our heads out of the blankets just this once? But I don't remember ever asking those questions.

I only remember being afraid every time Colonel Bob talked to the Indians, and I remember imagining the Mississippi River sparkling under the bridge in the summer sun. I suspect that I needed to believe in the west of Colonel Bob's imagination because it made the weekend bigger even than it was—big enough to fill up the other 363 days of the year that I spent more or less alone and afraid, waiting for the next trip to Apache Gulch.

Colonel Bob isn't around anymore, so I can't ask him, but I suspect he needed to believe in it too, or knew we needed it enough to keep the whole story going. It seems like I was nine or ten when Bethlehem got its first skyscraper, a thirteen-story building Bethlehem Steel built. In my memory, it looks like a giant I-beam, though I probably have that confused with an award they gave me for being an outstanding student, silver bookends in the shape of an I. There wasn't a place in town from which you couldn't see that building, not even down in the canyon, not even under the thick canopy of the trees in Apache Gulch.

The camping weekend rolled around that year and Colonel Bob spoke to the assembled children in his driveway.

"I'm getting too old to go all the way out west this year," he told us, "so this time we're going to go up to the Poconos. No need to ride under blankets, since it's such a short way, and the Indians are friendlier in those parts; they don't eat buck privates for lunch."

The trip to the Poconos took almost two hours, roughly five times longer than the trip to Apache Gulch, but Bob said it was shorter and with our heads out of the blankets we believed him. Colonel Bob preserved Apache Gulch for all of us, the only way he could have, by abandoning it once and for all.

I went camping with Colonel Bob for a total of fifteen years, even coming home from college twice to make the trip as a "grown-up" who got to drink beer and delegate. The highest rank I received: captain.

It's funny now, to think of those woods, ferny and moist, puddled and green, not a real mountain for a thousand miles, and to think that for years it was my idea of the west. Maybe that's why the west so bowled me over when I finally got here; maybe that's why I felt so much like I'd come home. In any case, I know I owe my love of the wilderness, and the fact that I did find my way home to the west, to a man who had never been here.

He always shook my hand just before I set out on the Bravery Test. While my flashlight searched the woods for markers, I could feel the lingering strength of his grip.

A Man Who'll Freeze
His Eyelashes for You

Of all the places on earth I love, there isn't one I love more than the canyons of southeastern Utah. It is Colorado Plateau country where the Colorado and the Green Rivers have swept through the sandstone, the wind and water working on the landscape for centuries until it has made thousands of square miles of buttes and mesas, of canyons that repeat into infinity, of rocks every color of sunburn working its way into tan, of shapes that at once excite and defy the imagination.

The Utah desert has always been home to many of the creatures who make a career out of being alone: coyotes, lizards, scorpions, tarantulas, golden eagles, and peregrine falcons. It used to be a good place for humans who liked to be alone too, until mountain-bike mania and the ecowarrior revolution set in. These days, in the summer, fall, and winter the desert looks more like a theme park than a wilderness as literally thousands of people a day come to ride jeeps and ATVs and bicycles in every direction. In an instant they destroy the delicate microorganism-rich surface of the soil called cryptogam that has taken decades to form and is the desert's built-in protection against erosion. They burn the rare piece of downed wood in their campfires, a scraggy piñon or a juniper bush that as many as ten different desert creatures depend upon for survival. They fill what was once a breathtakingly silent place with shrieks and war whoops and radios and the incessant sound of engines revving.

For me, the desert experience is one that demands isolation and silence. I want to look across the expanses of fifty or a hundred miles and see nothing but sunshine bouncing off rock. I want it to be so quiet I can hear the beating of the bats' wings as they swoop through the campground at twilight. I want to wake up alone in the middle of a blank space on the map that is bigger than my ability to imagine it, roll out of my sleeping bag, climb to the top of a rock and jump up and down naked till the sun warms me up. But it's getting harder and harder to find that isolation. Now if I want to be alone in the canyons I have to go when nobody else wants to: in the deepest, deadest heart of winter.

The day dawns clear and cold in Colorado while my boyfriend David and I load the car for the trip over the several mountain passes between my home and the Utah desert. When I say clear, I mean the air is so fine and sharp we can count the icicles hanging from the aspen trees on the mountainside two miles away; when I say cold, I mean in the neighborhood of forty below.

I assure David it will be much warmer in the lower elevation of the desert, but I'm careful not to say exactly *how* much. David is from New York, and though we have enough things in common that the relationship is off to a good start, wilder-

ness adventure isn't one of them. Just before we leave my driveway he admits to having never slept on the ground.

Because this is our first outdoor experience together, I want
everything to be perfect. Unfortunately for both of us, cold-
weather camping is by definition imperfect. The daytime
temperature can be bad enough, down around zero if a stiff
wind is blowing, and the nights are long . . . longer than anyone who has never spent a night out in one can possibly imagine, and the temperature can drop just as far as it wants
to—my worst night out ever was sixty below. What you do on
a night like that is burrow into your sleeping bag, head and all
like a groundhog, and lie awake observing how it feels as the
numbness moves from your extremities inward. You pray for
daylight. You don't ever go out to pee.

I know David isn't exactly sure why we are doing this. I
have told him about the winter light in the desert, low and
long and breathtaking as it bounces off the red rocks, lighting
them a color they never achieve during the rest of the year.
I've told him about the icicles that form in the hanging gardens, how magical the fairy-tale rock formations look with a
fresh dusting of pristine snow. I've told him that to experience
the desert truly, one must be alone there, that a pack of eighteen Boy Scouts on three-wheelers can ruin a desert day faster
than a dust storm, that the essence of the desert is silence,
meditation, empty spaces, and peace.

What I don't tell David is that in addition to all these sound
reasons, I am also driven by some questionable ones. Like how
I seem to need to put myself at risk in ways a lot like this once
a month or so just to remind myself that my blood is still
pumping, and that I love to show off my skills and equipment

a little more than I should. Nor do I tell him that in spite of all my tough talk, every time I enter nature when conditions are life-threatening, I'm more than a little scared.

It was a man very different from David who first taught me to love the desert. It was a man who spent all his time outdoors in extreme environments—the most windblown deserts, the most frigid tundra, the wildest rivers and remotest glaciers—and never thought to ask why. Like most outdoorsmen, he didn't talk much, and when I got to go along I knew I was meant not to talk much either, to ask only the rarest question, certainly never to complain. The tacit understanding was that everything had to be hard and painful to be good, so I baked and I shivered, got frostbite and windburn, went weeks without showers and toilets, fresh fruits and vegetables, even clean drinking water—months of physical discomfort and fear of exposure without knowing exactly what for. I can't be sure of all the reasons, but in time, I started to like it, and the longer I spent out there, the less I wanted to come back.

It's got something to do with returning to what's elemental . . . the pleasure of a whole day where the only thing you accomplish is what's essential for survival: taking a walk, building a fire, creating a shelter, making something to eat. Perhaps it's our need—almost forgotten—to immerse ourselves in the rare beauty of the natural world for more than a few hours and at its own pace and without a tinted windshield between it and us. And perhaps those of us who love it out there are a bit masochistic. I've never felt like I'm on vacation if there's not at least a little suffering involved.

Nowadays, there seem to be a lot of us out there: women who at one time followed men into the deep heart of the wilderness and then realized they didn't need those men to translate it for them, realized they understood it just fine on their own, realized that in the final analysis, those strong silent types don't have much to say except to tell you what and how often you do something wrong. So we left those men and bought our own outdoor equipment, became experts and guides instead of perennial apprentices, began to like our nature served up as wild and as hard as those men do. We spent a lot of years after that—or I did—dating men who lived in cities and read books, men who would no more sleep on the ground in the middle of winter than steal a car, and when we went back to the wild places we usually went alone.

Driving through this icy morning with David in the car, our two very different brands of antcipation about the weekend heavy in the air, I realize with some horror that I have become the strong silent type. Probably not as strong and hopefully not as silent as that man in my past, not as given to making things as hard and as dangerous as possible just for the sake of it, but the thought is enough to alert me to the danger of what I could become. I vow to encourage David to talk about his apprehension. I decide to do what I can to make us as comfortable as possible, and as safe.

We stop at the City Market in Moab and buy twenty gallons of water, some fruit, nuts, cheese, and chocolate for the trail, four cans of Chunky chicken soup, a box of instant mashed potatoes, and three bundles of firewood that look a little green to me. In the summer I like nothing better than to cook four-course dinners on my little Coleman stove: linguine with clam sauce or Chilean sea bass with Roma tomatoes, green onions and capers, hearts of palm and arugula salads and pineapple upside-down cake in the Dutch oven for dessert. When I'm winter camping the rules are as follows: dinner must be fast, hot, and filling, and contain nothing too complicated to be prepared in the dark.

By the time we get to Squaw Flat campground in the Needles District of Canyonlands National Park, it's nearly three o'clock in the afternoon. In spite of its offensive name, the flat is a beautiful place, a handful of campsites laid across and around a field of blond-and-red boulders, isolated well from the world and each other, a view to the south of the candy-striped pinnacles called the Needles, and to the north the massive mesa top called Island in the Sky.

The ranger comes by and gives us the bad news first: the temperature bottomed out last night at twenty-eight below zero. The good news is we are the only people "twisted enough" to try and camp out since the frigid Alaskan air mass arrived earlier in the week. My original thought was to hike in for a few hours before we made camp, but those temperatures are even worse than I expected, and if we sleep near the truck we'll have the option of jumping in and turning on the heater if hypothermia sets in.

Pitching my tent on a patch of red sand in front of a big blond piece of sandstone under a blue Utah sky has got to be one of the single greatest pleasures of my life. David is leaning against the truck watching me while I spring back and forth in the chilly afternoon air, popping the shock-corded poles together, shaping the yellow and blue of the tent around them, blowing up the Therm-a-Rests and fluffing up the sleeping bags, virtually overcome with delight.

We pick a hike for what little remains of the afternoon, up

Big Spring Canyon and back down Squaw Canyon, nearly eight miles in the less than two hours we've got left—including twilight. One more thing David doesn't yet know about me is how I love to push daylight, how Search and Rescue has several times been called out for me by a worried boyfriend at eleven or midnight, how they so far haven't found me because I've always managed to find my own way, precisely if slowly, by inching along the trail in the dark.

Big Spring Canyon is magical at this time of year; the water is frozen in pockets around cattails and bunch grass, and sheets of ice cascade down the rimrock waterfalls every several hundred yards. When the trail climbs up to the slickrock, frozen potholes gleam silver, dotting the golden surface of the rock like it's a giant piece of Swiss cheese. The late-afternoon light turns the rocks auburn, gold, and sienna. Then the sun sets and the temperature instantly drops fifteen degrees.

David is looking at his watch, and then the sky, a little too often. We're only halfway around the loop and Venus is already visible in the twilight sky. I pick up the pace a little on the way back down Squaw Canyon, which feels like a good strategy as the temperature continues to fall. By the time we reach the trailhead it's what most people would call pitch dark, but I'm an expert in the post-twilight glow that can last on a clear night as much as an hour. I find the last half mile of the trail by keeping my eyes on what's left of the glow on the western horizon and sensing, more than seeing, the slightly lighter swath of trail at my feet.

Back at camp, David is suitably impressed, and even more so when fifteen minutes later and out of total darkness I produce chicken soup nestled in a bed of mashed potatoes so hot he has to wait a few minutes before he can wolf it down.

One key to surviving a night out at subzero temperatures is to stay awake and active, to keep from going to bed for as long as you possibly can. When it gets dark at five-thirty, just making it to nine can feel like a feat. Since campfires have never been my forte, I assign that task to David, but the wood is green and we have very little kindling. The fire dwindles and sputters, and even when David manages to revive it, on his hands and knees blowing his lungs out for ten minutes, it still doesn't give off enough heat to make staying up and sitting around it worthwhile.

"Okay, Sheena of the desert," David says, "let's see what magic you can work here." It is an unfamiliar and not entirely unpleasant feeling being the macho half of a couple.

"I've been told that you always have to make a chimney," I say, separating two of the bigger logs in the suffocating fire with the toe of my boot, "like that."

Five more cold seconds tick by before the fire bursts into a full-fledged blaze, surprising nobody more than me.

"You crack me up," David says, warming his hands by the fire, and I think, *I hope he's still laughing at five a.m.*

The look he gives me when I tell him he'll be warmer if he takes all his clothes off before he gets into the sleeping bag is one I'll remember for the rest of my life. We are standing outside the tent shivering, the temperature hovering somewhere around zero, tonight's supply of firewood turned to embers, nowhere to go now but inside the tent. What I've told him is true. Sleeping bags around bare flesh hold heat; if you wear your sweaty clothes to bed you'll freeze within an hour. I've brought two Marmot bags, the very best design for cold-weather camping, and I've lined them with pile that I'm hoping will give us an extra ten or fifteen degrees.

"I haven't been wrong so far," I say, which is also true, unless you pause to consider why anybody would want to spend almost fifteen hours of darkness in temperatures that will stay above twenty below if we're lucky. A coyote calls from somewhere down the canyon and a great gray owl calls as if in answer from the trees at the mouth of Big Spring.

"Look at the stars," I say, now that we've lost the light from the fire. To say there are hundreds of thousands of them, to try to assign any number to their multitude, would be to understate how many there are.

"We are the only people," I say, "probably for three or four thousand square miles." I know as I say it that this detail about our condition might be enchanting only to me.

"No clothes at all," David says, and it's too dark for me to see if the look on his face is a smile or a grimace. We strip quickly and dive for the tent.

After David is snoring the fear I've been staving off sets in, most of it entirely unjustified. We are, after all, camped right next to my truck, which will in all likelihood start in spite of the cold if we wake up hypothermic and in serious trouble. Of course there's always the possibility we wouldn't wake up, that dementia would set in with the hypothermia and we wouldn't think of the truck, or that we'd wait too long before moving and our body temperature would drop so far and so fast that the urge toward sleep (that big final sleep) would be more than we could battle. Coyotes driven to insanity by winter hunger and insane-asylum escapees flit through my mind briefly, but fail to earn serious consideration in the face of the much more present adversary. That David will think I'm insane when he wakes up with no feeling from his knees down and demand that I drive him to the nearest airport fails to gain purchase either. Love me, I always say, love my perverse idea of a really good time.

I wake up once to find frost on everything: the tent wall, the sleeping bags, David's eyelashes. He is still sleeping, so I move my hand one millimeter at a time to unzip the window and check the position of the Big Dipper, knowing it will tell me the approximate time. My guess, after seeing it, is four-thirty, which is a pleasant surprise considering it's the first time I've awakened.

Three hours till daylight. Four hours till warmth we can feel. My fingers and toes have felt better, and I've got one of those headaches you get from eating ice cream too fast, but other than that my lined bag seems to be working. The next time I wake up there is light in the sky and David is watching me, all smiles, his face poked out of the top of his bag.

"Nothing to it," he says, unzipping his bag and pulling on layers of clothing. "I slept like a baby."

He is, I remember, the world's greatest metabolizer. I want to tell him to wait thirty minutes for sunrise before he commits to getting out of the tent, but I'm so happy he's happy I don't dare interrupt. We shiver over the coffeepot until the sun rises and the temperature bounces up so fast we can watch the mercury rise in our pocket thermometer, fifteen, then twenty, then thirty degrees.

Today's hike is world-class: back down Big Spring Canyon, then over to Druid Arch, across the Joint Trail to Chesler

Park—my favorite high meadow in all of Canyonlands—and then back across the slickrock to the campground. Even in summer, this hike makes for a long day, seventeen miles and quite a bit of it scrambling, so we set out early and at a pretty good clip. We run into trouble about five miles into the hike where the trail climbs up and over a big sandstone fin. Ice has formed in all the hand- and toeholds along the trail and though we give it several good tries, each one lands us hard on our butts at the bottom of the slickrock. We try circumventing that part of the trail, but as is always the case in the Canyonlands, the trail is laid where it is for a reason; it's the only possible way to get from point A to B.

I'm discouraged about missing Druid Arch, my favorite arch in all of southern Utah, but if we double back and keep moving we can still make Chesler Park by nightfall. How we'll get back to our campsite in the dark, I decide, is a bridge we'll cross when we come to it.

For the next few hours I become a little destination-obsessed (just one more thing David doesn't yet know about me) and I lead us at a half-trot through some of the world's most spectacular country, up and over big red fins of sandstone, along canyon rims every color from white to rust, squeezing through slot canyons so narrow we have to turn our hips to the side. By the time the sun starts to set I'm practically at a dead run, charging up a scree field and leaping over boulders, staying just far enough ahead of David so he can't say, "So how far is it then, really, back to camp?"

I have a plan that involves a quick drink of water and a ten-second view of Chesler Park at sundown, then a fast three miles down a trail I've never been on before that will take us to the end of a jeep road just under four miles from our camp. It's a longer route than the trail I intended, but four miles on a jeep road in total darkness is a better bet than two miles in the same conditions, climbing up and down ice-coated ridges where all day, off and on, we've had to use our hands.

The post-twilight glow gives us two of the three trail miles. David is having a hard time seeing well enough to stay with me but I won't let him take his headlamp out because the minute we do that our night vision is shattered for good. The trail markers, tiny piles of rocks called cairns along the side of the trail, seem close enough together in the daylight, but I know from experience they are out of headlamp range come nightfall.

I'm finding the trail now by one-tenth sight and nine-tenths intuition, sure that if I stop, even for a second, I'll lose my momentum and realize there's no earthly reason why I'm still moving through the blackness with relative ease. What we'll have to do once we admit it's really dark is stop at each cairn and send one person out in search of the next one. A mile could take hours at that rate. The slower we go the harder it will be to maintain body heat. There's always a chance we'll still walk up on an ice-covered ledge or a wall we can't negotiate. If that happens, I'm not sure what we'll do next.

Eventually, there's nothing to do but get out the headlamp, and my estimate of a half mile left on the trail turns out to be conservative. In only a few more cairns I can make out the reflective glint of an instruction sign that marks the end of the road. After the thin trail, the jeep road glows so brightly in the starlight that we relax along it as though it were daylight. By the time we get to camp we are ravenous and exhausted, and I set about making another instant-mashed-potato meal.

"You were amazing," David says. "Like some kind of bob-cat out there."

"That's why I'm here," I say. "For those thirty or forty min-utes I feel like a bobcat." But this time maybe I'm also here for something else. Maybe I'm here to witness David pass a great big love test with flying colors, and to realize that by making it as comfortable as possible, I may have passed a little one myself. Maybe I'm here to find out there's nothing more romantic than a man who will freeze his eyelashes for you and wake up with a smile on his face.

We eat our dinner silently, happily, as Orion climbs higher and higher in the sky. Tonight we'll sleep so hard we won't notice our freezing extremities, and neither of us will wake until the sun has warmed the tent. The temperature has fallen below zero degrees. The coyote calls from up-canyon but this time the owl doesn't answer. It hardly needs to be said that there is still no one in the campground but us.

one
long look
in the
mirror

―――――――

The Morality
of Fat

You know you've really lost weight, I've heard it said, when you actually weigh less than it says on your driver's license, the place where even people who are pathologically honest think it's okay to lie. As a writer, I make truth my business, and yet I'll admit right now that I have never told anyone how much I really weigh—not my best friend, not my mother, and, even when my life depended on it, not the hot-air balloon pilot or the man who tunes the bindings on my skis. I am a reasonably attractive, big-boned, tall, athletic, muscular woman, and I have struggled with my weight every day since my first conscious memory. I am one of the countless number of American women who go through fifteen-pound weight swings as often and as regularly as the moon goes through its phases. I set next-to-impossible weight-loss goals for myself and feel devastated when I don't meet them, ecstatic when occasionally I do. But truth and lies, devastation and ecstasy sound like the stuff of careers and relationships. Why do we waste so much of that kind of energy thinking about how much we weigh?

There was a time in my life—actually, most of my life—when I couldn't have written this essay, a time in my life when if anyone had even suggested that I would be a good person to write about weight control, I would have flown into silent rage and self-loathing.

I made up my mind to write this essay cocky and firm at the bottom end of my fifteen-pound cycle. I am getting around to writing it, now, frightened and dangerously close to the top. And I can't go any further without saying what has to be said: At the bottom of my cycle I weigh 145 pounds and I am reasonably happy (albeit daydreaming about the next five pounds); at the top, 160, I am cranky, depressed, and oversensitive about everything. If you know anything about the psychology of weight loss, you'll also know that this is true: Writing that last sentence is the hardest thing I've done all year.

Like me, most women in America are obsessed with being thin, and also like me, thin is something most of those women will never be. We support a thirty-billion-dollar diet industry in this country, and a discouraging 98 percent of us gain back all of the pounds we diet to lose. The National Institutes of Health has proved that diets don't work (as if we didn't know), and at least one respected expert in eating disorders disputes the establishment's belief that excess weight causes health problems. "There are no studies proving that weight causes disease," Dr. Susan Wooley of the University of Cincinnati says. "The predilection to certain diseases could well cause the extra weight."

Why, then, do we refuse to accept and enjoy our bodies the way they are? Why do thinness and fatness line up so exactly with good and evil in the marketplace, the media, and the social circles of our lives? Why is a thin person automatically assumed to be happier, more confident, and more in control of her life than a fat person? Why do our heroes, our superstars, our role models, even our wished-for body shapes keep getting thinner and thinner? (From Venus de Milo to Kristin Scott Thomas is a long, fatophobic way.) If there is an ideal body weight, why do people on one side of the line get so much poorer treatment than those on the other? Why isn't anyone ever discriminated against for being too thin?

I was having lunch with a friend, another warrior in the battle of fifteen-pound weight swings. She was at the bottom of her cycle, was moving on down from it to a new all-time low. She hadn't weighed as little as she weighed that day at lunch since the tenth grade. "I just don't want one more person to tell me how good I am," she said through clenched teeth. "I was just as good as I am now when I weighed one hundred and seventy; I won't be any more good at one thirty-five. I'm not sure what it takes to do this," she said, "but goodness has very little to do with it."

Another friend has gained thirty or forty pounds recently. "People keep asking me what's wrong," she told me, "as if the extra pounds are some sort of manifestation of an underlying tragedy in my life. The fact is that everything is going so well in my life that I decided to relax a little bit about the weight thing, not make it such a big deal anymore."

I listened to my friend and tried to imagine what it would be like to relax about my weight a little, what it would be like to buy an article of clothing just because I liked it, without worrying whether or not it made me look thin, what it would be like to go into the ski shop and tell the binding technician the truth. Is one of my friends smarter than the other; is either any more good?

To my parents, it seemed to me, appearance was weight. "How's your weight?" my mother always asked, sometimes before "How are you?" when we were living in separate states. The next two questions were "How's your face?" and "How's your hair?" but they diminished, exponentially, in importance. Generally accepting of my every imaginative or intellectual oddity, what my mother most feared was an overweight child. My parents spoke in whispers about their friends' kids who were overweight, not only as if they had a deadly disease but worse, as if they had willed it on their parents somehow, disgraced them purposefully.

I was rewarded for losing weight with clothes and makeup, and for gaining weight I was shamed into staying in my room during meals. I am the only child I have ever known who got bubble bath and face cleanser in her Easter basket instead of chocolate.

Once, my little group of fourth-grade friends, in a typical gesture of childhood cruelty, formed a club and wouldn't let me in. They sent me notes that said "No fat people allowed" and "Fat is where it's at, so you'll do fine." In a childhood out of which I remember very little, I can still see the uneven handwriting on those bits of paper; I can still see my mother, terrified, angry, her eyes wild with concern.

When I look at preteen and teenage photos of myself, I see a kid in a halter top and cutoffs, not skinny exactly, but looking like every other thirteen-year-old kid. Age and distance have made me understand that I wasn't, in reality, any fatter than the little girls who wrote the note, but what they could see was the weak spot in my self-perception. I thought I was immense, a walking houseboat, a bag of chocolate-chip cookie dough with legs. I believed not only that I was fat but also that the fatness was the outward exhibition of something terrible inside me. When somebody who wasn't fat liked me, I thought it was a miracle. I was, and still in some ways am, intimidated by all those thin people in the world—cheerleaders and prom queens, most significantly—who I believed must be filled with goodness.

Desperate to please my parents and terrified more than anything of being called fat, I started walking the line I'm still walking thirty years later: the 145-pound me, healthy and strong and very attractive in carefully chosen clothing, and the 160-pound me, someone who would be pretty if only . . . My mother believed, with every bit of her heart, that if only I was thinner, I would have more and better friends, I would be accepted into a more competitive college, and, most recently, I would sell more copies of my book of short stories.

And maybe the saddest part of this whole story is that my mother turns out to be at least partially right. I could make a long list of behaviors, actual scientifically proven differences between the way people treat me at 145 and the way they treat me at 160. I could start with the men, but it's not only them; sometimes the cruelest treatment comes from the other women who are just as afraid of being fat as I am.

"People never forget what you look like the first time they see you," my mother always said. "And if what they see is a fat girl, then that is what you'll always be." There are some days when I'm pretty sure that I'm not a fat girl; there are other days—more of them—when I'm sure I am. My mother's greatest fear has become so much my own that even now, when I look in the mirror, I can't see what I look like. I will never have any realistic idea about whether I am fat or not.

I know there are countless professionals of varying reliability out there to help me restructure my relationship to food and weight control, but here at 158 pounds and holding, this is how it seems to me: I will never put a piece of food in my mouth without feeling guilty; I will never look in the mirror and feel okay about my body; and I will never, ever be at a weight, no matter how much I might one day lose, that I will consider ideal.

"I can do everything I want to do," says the ad for Jenny Craig Weight-Loss Centers, "except keep off extra weight," and isn't it a mystery indeed? In just one year of my life I managed to get a book of short stories published, run seven of the country's most difficult rivers, lead a photographic safari in Africa, and teach a bunch of eighteen-year-old Mormon students to love poetry. Surely keeping off fifteen pounds can't be harder than all that.

The only bad review my book of short stories received was from a man who conceived of himself as a cowboy even though what he actually did was sell textbooks in the midwest. (I know this because, after trashing my book, he sent me a picture of himself in full cowboy regalia with a letter asking for a date.) The review was bad, the headline worse, but the only line I remember went like this: *Can an overweight, over-sexed easterner find happiness in the west?* And it's not the over-sexed part that sticks.

Old insecurities die hard. Even to this day, call me stupid and I'll laugh in your face; call me a bad writer and I'll discuss art with you all day long; but call me fat and you'll send me sobbing to the bathroom, and I'll wear tent dresses for the next six days.

I spent one winter in Ohio and had the good fortune to be taken in and looked after by a wonderful family of big women. Aware of my loneliness and able to cut through my defenses, these women made me feel welcome in my weekly visits to their house, where we, among other things, got naked together and sat in the hot tub and howled at the moon. Being the fourth person in a hot tub with three of these women made me feel tiny and, for a moment, thin, but before too long I realized it also made me feel invisible, insignificant, and hung up on extremely unimportant things. I will tell you that these women were beautiful (they were, you can believe me or not), their big white bodies illuminated by moonlight, silver bubbles all around them—but even more than they were beautiful, they were good.

Is it better to be thin than fat? Is it better to be thin than good? Is there a morality of fat, and if so, on which side of the line does self-acceptance fall? Will I ever stop measuring my self-worth according to whether I wear a size 10 or 14? Or will I starve myself for the next three or four weeks so that I'll lose fifteen pounds by the time anybody reads this essay? Most likely, I'm sorry to say, it will be the latter. Still, the longer, more difficult path to goodness and the acceptance that comes with it has to be, I think, the ultimate goal. I'll never look like Kristin Scott Thomas (though God knows I would love to), so I guess the Venus de Milo will have to be a more realistic role model for me.

In Pursuit of What
I Don't Do Well

A journalist named Karen called and asked if she could do an interview. "In your element," she said. "You pick the time and place." My element, that week, was southern Utah's San Juan River, where I was leading a beginner's whitewater rafting class. I asked her to come along.

As we floated down the gray, silty river between the mineral-stained canyon walls, the relatively easy class 2 rapids behind us, Karen got out her camera, notebook, and pen.

We talked about my life. How I've made the large chunk of land between Salt Lake City and the Grand Canyon my backyard, my temple; how I spend at least half of every year outside.

"And where do you get all your athletic ability?" Karen asked.

I laughed out loud. "I don't have any," I said. "This is all an act."

And it is true. For all the things I undertake—whitewater rafting, backpacking, rock climbing, skiing, scuba diving, tennis, kayaking, horseback riding, softball, sailing, etc.—I have not one ounce of natural ability. God gave me brains, a good ear for language, a face that most people think they can get along with, and my mother's strong legs. Grace, finesse, timing, and all the other things that make an athlete an athlete didn't come in my package.

"You've got to give Pam credit," my athletic friends and lovers have always said about me. "She'll try just about anything." And this too is true. Year after year, season after season, I find myself guiding a raft down the country's most dangerous white water, skiing the trees next to the double-black-diamond runs, urging a horse that is way too strong over a series of jumps that are way too high, and not looking particularly graceful at any of it. I am relentless in my pursuit of what I don't do well, and I will stop at almost nothing.

Do I enjoy it? A lot of the time, mostly between outings, I think so. But in the heat of the moment I spend a lot of time making deals with the deity that governs athletic pursuits. "Please God, don't let there be an avalanche; please God, don't let my foot slip; and please God, don't let them hit the ball toward me in right field. If you just get me down off this ledge this one time I promise I will never . . ." I am not, I know, a total klutz. If I were, given the things I have tried, I'd be dead.

For my father, beauty and athletic ability are one and the same. When he looked at me as a child and saw neither, he turned his attention to other things: his business, the ball game, Chris Evert on TV. Beauty, I learned, was not something that could be attained in still life; the only true beauty was beauty in motion. Peggy Fleming dipping her lovely body toward the toe of her ice skate; Olga Korbut, weightless, mid-cartwheel on the gymnasium floor; a Dallas Cowboys cheer-leader kicking high above her feathered hair; and Chris Evert—most of all, Chris Evert—tossing, reaching, lunging toward her serve.

My father wanted me to be a tennis player more than he wanted anything in the world. A natural athlete himself, he tried to coach me. "Move your feet!" I can still hear him shout from the other side of the net. "Follow through!" It was the one thing he ever tried to teach me, the one thing we really could have shared. As with everything else, I was only mar-ginally good at tennis. I tripped and sweated my way to my first and only trophy, handed my father my racket, and vowed never to play tennis again.

What the trophy actually signified has gotten a little hazy over the years. My father says I won first place in the country club's fourteen-and-under singles tournament. In my mother's version I was *runner-up* in the *city's* fourteen-and-under tour-nament. But I've carried that trophy around with me for a lot of years, and it doesn't say first place or runner-up. The words carved into the square plate underneath the arching gold fig-ure read "Fourteen and Under: Most Improved."

If tennis were really only tennis, it would have been okay to be "most improved," but tennis was everything. It was grace, it was style, it was beauty, and at fourteen the lesson I learned was simple: Without it, I wouldn't be attractive to a man. Beauty wasn't something I wanted to be "most improved" at. And when I put down my racket "forever," it must have looked like I was admitting defeat. But in truth, I just needed a different weapon. In truth, I had not yet begun to fight.

———

I'm told that most women get their idea of beauty from their mothers, and I think of all the broken bones I could have saved myself (seven, not even counting ribs) had the things that made my mother beautiful been enough for me. My mother, an actress, was drop-dead gorgeous in poster-size promotion pictures that gather dust on my parents' basement walls. She tried to teach me a whole other type of beauty: what clothes to buy and how to wear them, how to put on makeup, where to part my hair. When I do all this according to her instructions, which I do about twice a year, people tell me I am beautiful, and I believe them. But this is a different kind of beauty, and because it comes too easily, because it comes at all, I don't trust my relationship to it: it feels like I am pulling off some kind of gag.

Becoming beautiful for my mother meant an hour's worth of fun at the mirror, a trip to the masquerade party, getting to be the princess on Halloween. Becoming beautiful for my father is a self-imposed sentence, an M. C. Escher drawing: the lizard eternally climbing the infinite stairs. My mother's definition of beauty is as far away as stardust; my father's as close as my heartbeat, as real as a broken bone. So in a way that now strikes me as infuriatingly predictable, I turned my young adult life into a series of athletic endeavors, mostly in the path of men who were much too handsome and astonishingly athletic: ex–skiing coaches, world-class kayakers, international rugby players.

The men I met in pursuit of my own athleticism led me to places I probably had no business being. The most stunning example of this is the three seasons I spent guiding hunters in

Alaska. Somehow I believed that climbing those mountains for eighteen and sometimes twenty hours a day, wet and cold and hungry, would make me feel beautiful in the eyes of the man I loved, the guide I shared a base camp with. It wasn't exactly tennis, but in my mind it became a new means to old ends: sweat, strength, muscle, motion. I would have a natural beauty, I thought, a beauty that would transcend no showers, no makeup, no clothes except for camouflage fatigues, no cream rinse, no earrings. And I was right. I never looked as beautiful to that man as I did near the end of those eight weeks, tanned and strong and dirty. Almost as beautiful as the next girl he would see back in civilization walking down the street.

Another man and I would go skiing. All the way up to the top: the double-black-diamonds called Jupiter Bowl. We would spend the day up there, him cutting perfectly symmetrical turns through the powder, me behind, crossing his first three, maybe four turns and then catching an edge and falling, somersaulting, plummeting, skis and poles flying in all directions, snow packing down into my face, my ski suit, my boots. And then we would go back and do it again. One day I was fifteen minutes late for the therapy this pursuit had sent me into because after nine collarbone-wrenching, knee-twisting falls I felt I had to go up the lift one more time. I guess I thought I might, against all odds, get it right, my skis cutting his turns into perfect figure eights, my arms and legs bending and lifting, shooting feathery arcs of powder behind me, my face brilliant, shining in the ice-cold sunlight: beautiful.

Would it have been possible in those days for me to fall in

love with a paunchy man, bookish and kind, who took his idea of beauty more from a Renaissance painting than from a Coors Light commercial? Not one chance in a million.

There were other men, all more or less the same, so when I met the man who would turn out to be my husband, nobody was surprised to find out that he was an African safari guide. But there was one difference. Very beautiful and athletic himself, Mike had an eye for inner beauty that can only have come from a life far away from American commercialism and pageantry. He had an appreciation for a well-cooked meal, for a quick imagination, and for movies with happy endings (he nods his head vigorously when the characters do the right thing). He thinks Sally Field is the most beautiful woman alive. When his best man told him he wanted to have a bachelor party with naked dancing girls jumping out of a cake, Mike said, "What kind of cake?"

I took Mike to Alaska to show him our version of the Kalahari—the place where I used to lead hunters, a place I have come to love and, like the Utah desert, think of as home. Another couple came along. Julia was graceful and quick, a woman who actually got more beautiful each day she didn't have a shower; her husband was a little slow and awkward, like me.

On the day we decided to climb the steep rock moraine on the side of an isolated mountain glacier, it became clear that two of us were acrophobic and two of us were not. While Mike and Julia scrambled up the moraine like mountain goats, Ted and I hung back, whining, clinging, becoming alternately angry and hysterical, putting our bodies into one awkward position after another. My acrophobia is something I confront often, and eventually I always make it, hand over hand, up the face of the rock.

But it is in these moments—when my fingers leave one crack and reach for the next, when my weight falls forward on my skis at the edge of the cornice, when the fast water above the rapid tugs at the nose of my boat, when the long fly ball is coming toward me—that I ask myself, *Why am I not somewhere else doing something I am good at, like writing, for instance, or taking standardized tests, or growing vegetables, or playing the piano?* And the answer is, I must believe that one day I'll get it right. One day, if I try hard enough, I'll look like a woman on the cover of *Outside* magazine, like an ABC sports-highlights cut-to-commercial still, like a poster on the wall of a bar with too many TVs. I will be frozen there in the motion of someone's memory, and that someone (a man, my father, myself) will say, "That was beautiful!"

Out of Habit,
I Start Apologizing

I am lying, facedown, on a massage table at the Doral Hotel and Spa in Telluride, Colorado. I am here under false pretenses, a guest of the Doral and all its services, because the manager hopes I will write a rave article about the hotel. Because of his generosity, I am having several things that I cannot even pronounce done to my body for free. I've been bathed, oiled, rolfed, fangoed, facialed, shiatsued, reflexologized, stretched, pressed, and dried. More people have seen my naked body in the last three days than in the last three years, and I'm starting to get used to it, my modesty slipping away. I've begun to float from personal service room to personal service room in a fragrant, supple semiconsciousness. So far I've lost three hotel bathrobes, two sweatshirts, and my watch.

It is unlike me to have so much attention paid to my body, to pamper and indulge this fleshy mass that I have spent my whole life trying to reduce, or reshape, or disguise.

I'm being worked on, this hour, by a technician whose nametag says "Wendy," and she's doing something to me called the Rosen method, a loose combination of body massage and psychotherapy. Considering the fact that every insecurity I have ever harbored has had to do with the shape of my body, the Rosen method seems like the ideal treatment for me.

"You have such strong legs," Wendy says, "but you are using them to hold up the rest of your body, and that's not what they are for."

My legs are strong and beautiful; dancer's legs, my mother's legs: she spent a lifetime developing sinewy, shapely leg muscles, and then gave them, like a promise, to me.

"You are pulling your body up with your shoulders," Wendy says, "pushing and pulling, when you should only be supporting; no wonder everything is too tight."

I try to imagine standing without legs, or staying erect without shoulders, but quickly give up. I am already fantasizing about next hour's foot massage when Wendy says, "Is there some good reason you've convinced the rest of your body that your hips and stomach and pelvis don't even exist?"

When I was younger, I used to believe that if I were really thin I would be happy, and there is a part of me that still believes it's true. For a good part of my life I would have quite literally given anything to be thin . . . a finger, three toes, the sight in one eye. Now I find it only mildly surprising that for the majority of my lifetime I would have traded being pretty, whole, and fat for being ugly, deformed, and thin.

I am boating the whitewater section of the upper Dolores River at flood stage. With me in my sixteen-foot inflatable raft are three beautiful Texan women who literally can't fathom my strength. We are approaching an obstacle in the river known simply as the Wall, a place where almost the entire volume of water rushes into a huge sandstone monolith, dives under it, skims along its base, and comes out, frothy and white, on the other side.

Sneaking around the wall without hitting it requires lots of anticipation and, at this high river level, almost superhuman strength. A hundred yards downriver from me I see my husband's boat career closer and closer to the wall; I see one of his passengers disappear under the lip of the boat's front tube, the other two dive behind him into the river's swirl. When his boat makes contact with the sandstone I hear the splintering of wood, see an oar fly high into the air, taste the sudden rush of adrenaline in the back of my mouth.

My husband is the strongest human being I know, but I have the advantage of being second. I pull on the oars harder than I've ever pulled before, completely alert, making every stroke count. A voice that I recognize as mine tells my crew to get down on the floor of the raft, but I am not conscious of making the command. Every synapse in my brain and every muscle in my body is focused on pulling away from that wall. My feet, my thighs, my stomach, my back, my arms, my hands all work together, in a movement that is, I think, very like a wave, to bring the oars upstream against the rushing water. The wall gets closer and closer, and just when I think I am doing no good at all I feel the boat responding, moving backward against the current that's been driving it toward the rock. The nose of the boat barely kisses the wall and one more stroke pulls us safely away.

"Damn," says one of the Texans. "Hot damn."

We go to work rescuing the other boat's passengers.

I am walking down the street in Manhattan, Fifth Avenue in the lower Sixties, women with shopping bags on all sides. I realize with some horror that for the last fifteen blocks I have been counting how many women have better and how many women have worse figures than I do. Did I say fifteen blocks? I meant fifteen years.

I am sitting at my parents' dinner table in the summer between my freshman and sophomore years. I have brought the first boy I have ever really cared about home from college, and we are making vaguely interesting small talk while my mother portions out the food.

I have been at college so long I have forgotten the rules by which my family eats dinner. I am not allowed to have bread, dessert, or seconds, ever, and there is an especially tricky rule that has to do with how much money has been spent on dinner and whether I am, or am not, supposed to finish everything that's been put on my plate.

My young boyfriend is telling a story, rather unsuccessfully, that I know to be funny; I'm embarrassed for him, and I absentmindedly reach for a second helping of peas.

"You start eating like that," my father barks at me, "and before too long you'll be as big as a house."

I stare at the spinach coagulating on my plate.

The trick has always been to look only selectively into the mirror. To see the bright eyes, the shining hair, the whispered print of the blouse falling open to reveal soft tanned cleavage, the shapely curve of a taut muscular calf.

My husband manages a restaurant here in town. He employs fifteen twenty-one-year-olds from California. They are all variations on blonde, on tan, on figures drawn to perfection. They call my husband Mick Dundee (after the movie about the human crocodile), which I find particularly revolting; they are the kind of girls who can't talk to a man without touching him. When I come to the restaurant they smile at me politely, curiously, something between wonder and doubt in their eyes. My husband, who is blond and tanned, and also built to perfection, says they do this because I am a published author, but I secretly believe they are trying to imagine what he could possibly see in someone with a body like mine.

My thinnest friend Kris says, "I don't know, but it seems to me that if the only thing that's wrong with you is that you weigh too much, you actually have it pretty good."

"The only thing?" I say to her, calmly. "The only thing?"

I am helicopter skiing in Idaho with a man named John that I, for no good reason at all, feel the need to impress. Six inches of snow have fallen just after midnight, and under those six inches there's a thick sun-ruined crust. The helicopter leaves us on the dark side of the Tetons. The man I am here with was born in the Sun Valley Lodge; he could ski before he was confidently walking. We are neither lovers nor quite yet friends. We find ourselves on top of this mountain together, practically by accident. And yet I need to ski well in front of him, and that need is almost enough to keep me from being scared.

John hops off the cornice and into the pristine bowl as if he's stepping off a sidewalk, as if it wasn't almost ninety degrees vertical, as if the sun wasn't hitting it and making it tetchy for avalanche, as if there wasn't that crustiness trying to grab his skis from underneath.

My last thought is, *The sooner I go, the less time he'll have to watch me*, so I launch myself, trying to find a rhythm, trying to make figure eights out of his perfect turns. The crust beneath the powder makes a terrible noise as it grips and releases, grips and releases, but I keep turning, thinking about weighting and unweighting my body, thinking about keeping my shoulders in the fall line, thinking about the ever-reliable strength in my knees.

I ski without my normal worst-case scenario tape playing in my head, although here there's more justification for it than usual. I ski way too fast, take too many chances; I become what the ski bums call *focused*, believing entirely in my body's ability to perform correctly, to absorb the slope's imperfections, to ride out the speed. I feel strangely light and incredibly agile, the turns becoming the downbeat in a song it feels like I could play forever. I ski past John, who has stopped to wait for me in a small grove of trees. The tails of my skis send up an arc of powder that coats him, and when I finally stop, ten perfect turns later, his head is thrown back in laughter and he looks like an angel in the snow.

"Hold your tummy in," my mother would yell every morning from the front door as I walked across the lawn to the waiting school bus, as if the bus didn't have open windows, as if what she really meant was goodbye.

My friends Terilynn and thin Kris and I are sitting in a coffee bar talking. I tell them about the girls at Mike's restaurant. Kris tells me I'm crazy, that I have an unrealistic view of my appearance, that those girls would never think such a thing, looking at me. Terilynn, who is imperfectly shaped in several of the same ways I am, is not quite so convinced.

"You're wrong," I tell Kris. "I have a perfectly reasonable idea of my own attractiveness . . . good legs, shiny eyes, a pretty face, nice hair. . . . On an attractiveness scale of one to a hundred, I'm in the high seventies, and ten pounds thinner, the mid-eighties."

"So what am I?" Kris says.

Both Terilynn and I put her in the high nineties, with a parenthetical reference to the fact that women, coveting her extreme thinness, might put her slightly higher than men.

We give Terilynn a seventy-two, with a high-eighties incentive if she continues to lose weight.

From there we get a little crazy, rating everyone from Jodie Foster (ninety-one) to Bill Clinton (eighty-four) to Gerard Depardieu (eighty-nine) to Madonna (upon whom we were unable to reconcile, the number ranging from twenty-seven to seventy-eight).

"This is the nineties, girls," the waitress says when she brings us the check. "We're supposed to be into inner beauty now."

Sometimes I'm afraid the main reason I spend half of my life outdoors is simply because there aren't any mirrors.

I'm sitting on my front porch, blank computer screen in front of me, except two words at the top: The body. I am determined to write something positive, having sworn not to spend as much of the second half of my life preoccupied with my physical imperfections as I did the first. A woman walks up the street, bone-thin in a running bra, Lycra shorts, and a Walkman. I look down at my shapeless flannel nightgown, my fuzzy slippers, my belly, my hips, and turn my computer off for at least an hour. The woman is striding big confident strides up my street, which is the steepest in our mountain town. She looks as if she will keep that pace right up and over the mountain.

I am hiking to the top of Mount Timpanogos, the highest mountain in my part of Utah, 11,750 feet above sea level, 5,340 above the trailhead where four hours ago I parked my car. Hiking Timpanogos is not scary or life-threatening, it's just grueling, roughly equivalent to starting on the rim of the Grand Canyon and then walking *up* one vertical mile to the river.

The only time safety on Timpanogos becomes an issue is in a sudden summer thunderstorm, when the shale that makes up the last hour of the climb turns slippery and loose, and lightning strikes the part of the mountain that's above the tree line, which for the hiker who gets stranded up there can amount to hours and hours of dodging the heart of the storm.

Today there is only blue sky on my side of the mountain, not so much as a cumulus cloud. Maybe that is why I'm so surprised when I arrive at the summit and see the other half of the sky, horror-film black and crackling with thunder and lightning, sheets of rain like iron curtains walking toward me from a storm center only a few hundred yards away.

The way I see it I have two choices: I can either pick my way between the lightning bolts for a couple of hours and risk a shaley mudslide under combined pressure of the rain and my weight, or I can leap down off the ridge of this mountain and into one of the permanent snowfields that line the mountain's steeper, "unclimbable" side. I won't have to stop exactly, just stay on my feet and do a little boot skiing for maybe ten minutes and a couple of thousand feet down to the bottom of the ice field and tree line. If I lose my footing and start rolling, my problems become a little more complex. I tighten down the straps on my daypack, find the shallowest part of the slope above which to get airborne, and count to three.

On two and a half I realize that no matter how hard I try to find one, there is no scenario of liking my body when it is stationary, no scenario that doesn't take place in a moment of life-or-death athleticism, of do-or-die strength.

I am lying on another table, face up this time, staring at the monkey my gynecologist has pasted to the ceiling to prove he has the sense of humor his schedule doesn't often allow him to show. He is a decent man, direct and gentle, but this is Utah, where men still own women's bodies, so the bills come to my house in some long-since-departed boyfriend's name.

We have our usual birth-control conversation. "What do you get when you cross Dan Quayle with an IUD?" I ask him, and he just shakes his head. I can't help myself. There's something about being in the gynecologist's office that turns me, instantly, into a stand-up comedienne.

This is the big 3-0 visit. A complete physical, my yearly pelvic, and because I have family history, the first mammogram of my life. The doctor broods over something he doesn't like in my folder while the nurse makes me get on the scale. Out of habit, I start apologizing, though the number turns out to be slightly lower than last year.

"There's something here that troubles me," the doctor says. "Just wait here a minute while I go call the lab."

"Where's he think I'm gonna go dressed like this?" I say to the nurse, but my voice cracks apart at the end like a mirror, my humor shot through with brittle fear. It has been less than a month since my best friend died of cancer, less than a year since my mother died of a heart attack, or long-term starvation, or the sheer displeasure of living with the things her aging body did.

No diagnosis yet and already the regret is settling in. I should have loved my body better, should have loved its curves and folds and softness, should have practiced standing with my pelvis the way Wendy told me to. But instead I have ignored it, left the cancer to grow in its dark uninhabitable recesses; I think of the drawer that holds my summer T-shirts, where every dark winter the mice move in.

When the nurse leaves the room I pull the hospital gown to one side and look down at myself, the inch of extra flesh on each hip, the way my belly pushes out in a particularly annoying way that makes the occasional bystander ask me if I'm pregnant.

A wave of love for my body that is as unfamiliar as it is terrifying washes over me. I'm afraid at first it is desperation love, the kind I've felt for a man only on the brink of his leaving, but this is more penetrating, all-encompassing; a love so sad and deep and complicated I am left, for a change, without words. I can almost feel the cancer spreading now, one cell at a time through the dark parts of me, and I stand alone in front of the mirror, trying to love it away.

The doctor opens the door and smiles, apologetic. "My mistake," he says, appearing not to notice my nakedness. "You're as healthy as an ox."

"How healthy is an ox?" I say, remembering a *National Geographic* special about oxen getting bugs up their noses that made them go insane, but the doctor is already out the door and with the next patient.

I let my legs go loose and try to stand using only my pelvis. I drop my shoulders as low as they will go and try to think about transferring my body weight (this takes tremendous concentration) to my hips. I take one more long look in the mirror before putting on my clothes.

Redefining
Success

I am walking along Muir Beach, twenty miles north of San Francisco, with my friend the poet Jane Hirshfield. It is a windy day, sunny and cold, the sea full of the memory of a storm that blew through last night.

My friendship with Jane is two years and a few dozen beach walks, horseback rides, and mud baths old. The relationship is deeply successful, like, *she* would say, the relationship between these huge dark rocks and the silver waves that crash all around them. I bring Jane my wild tales of failed love and adventure, my passion and spontaneity, my questions about how to live my life. She meets these with a hard-won wisdom as rich and as peaceful as the pear trees in her garden, a wisdom gained from years of sitting on a small pillow in a huge Buddhist monastery, a calm I can only covet while my life tosses itself from storm to storm.

When I moved to San Francisco, I was running, in the same moment both toward and away. Away from a life that had become stale and repetitive, away from a place where when I said "creative writing" everyone thought I meant calligraphy, away from a desert landscape that I loved more deeply than any I had loved before. What I ran toward was less certain: a big city, a new love, an imagined community of artists, the Pacific Ocean, organic vegetables, and exotic food.

But the love went bad and the ocean was frigid, and in less than a year in the land of milk and honey I was stalked, sued, threatened, abandoned, and mugged, twice. For the first time in my life I was afraid to go home at night, and I found myself alone as I had never been, in the way we never are until we are alone in the midst of five million people. It was from that city-solitude I began the tough work of reinventing my life, and now each talk with Jane clears a little more fog away.

Today we are talking about redefining success. I am telling her about my first notion of success, which came from my parents and involved country clubs, clothing, and cars. As I became an adult I replaced that list with a list of my own, no less arbitrary: a Ph.D., a book of short stories, a place on a best-seller list, a film. But now I am coming to the understanding that success has less to do with the accumulation of things and more to do with an accumulation of moments, and that creating a successful life might be as simple as determining which moments are the most valuable, and seeing how many of those I can string together in a line.

Jane asks me to give her examples, and I start with the easy ones first. The day I found out my book manuscript was accepted for publication, the time I heard one of my stories read aloud on NPR. But there was also last Tuesday morning, when something clicked together for my three-year-old horse, Deseo, and me and he didn't put his head down in defiance the way he had a hundred times before. And there was last month in Paris when my wallet and passport and all my credit cards got stolen, and I had an international flight in four hours, and it was a national holiday, and the guys at the police precinct pretended to have even a harder time than they should have had understanding my marginal French. But I made it to the airport with minutes to spare, some U.S. Embassy petty cash and a brand-new passport in my pocket, and enough residual adrenaline to lift the plane off the ground.

Then there are the moments when the challenge is less obvious, like the quiet end of the day telling stories with friends on the third night of a five-day river trip, the dishes done, the tents set up, everybody's real life a half a world away. Or each moment of conversation in the course of a day when I am able to do the one thing I most want to: speak from a place of courage and love instead of a place of insecurity and fear.

"Or this moment right now," I say to Jane, watching two dogs circle each other on the sand in front of us. "This conversation. This place."

"And what else?" Jane says.

"What else," I say, knowing her Zennish mind, "is that the moments of failure are important too. That if I'd fallen off the horse, or missed the airplane, or when I'm in one of those moments when fear consumes me, when I'm all alone on Sunday morning and it's the twenty-seventh straight day of rain . . . all those moments of struggling are important too, not just to provide the contrast, but because they use different muscles. They let me know I'm alive in a whole different way."

At this, Jane smiles.

"And what else?" she says.

I watch the ocean tumble onto the beach in front of us. I consult three pairs of gray gulls overhead.

"I don't know what else," I say.

But in my heart I *do* know. The "what else" is language: poems and stories, letters and scripts, the way every minute of my life that matters translates itself into the words that I write, the way the writing sanctifies the best times and makes the darkest times possible to bear. I am writing every moment I am living: as my loaded dogsled speeds across the north slope of the Brooks Range, as the man I finally get the nerve to ask out turns me down, as the minister tamps the ground over my mother's ashes, each morning as the sun first hits the waters of the San Francisco Bay.

My need to write the things that terrify me is matched only by my desire to write the things that surprise and delight. I take what the world hands me in free verse and give it back in something like a form and it is language that lets me complete that circle; it is quite literally the tether that keeps me connected to the earth. Sometimes I feel like a cannibal. Sometimes I wish there were five minutes of my life I didn't reinvent as I went along.

"What kind of beast would turn its life into words?" Jane says, quoting Adrienne Rich. Jane knows Rich's poems are to me as essential as clean water, so I smile and quote back:

"No one sleeps in this room without / the dream of a common language."

Tonight we will attend an awards ceremony where Rich will receive the Bay Area's Cody Award for lifetime achievement in the literary arts. In her most recent book of poems, *An Atlas of the Difficult World*, there is a poem about dislocation, where the poet finds herself in California, almost to her surprise. *This is no place you ever knew me*, the poem says, describing *small canyons running through pitched hillsides / liveoaks twisted on steepness, the eucalyptus avenue leading / to the wrecked homestead, the fog wreathed heavy-chested cattle / on their blond hills.*

I have read that poem each night since I have been in California, feeling a vicarious connection to this place through the poem's words and images, imagining the day when I will find solace in this landscape too. *This is where I live now*, the poem reminds me nightly. It has been my version of saying my bedtime prayers.

I have never seen Adrienne Rich read in person, so I sit beside Jane at the award ceremony so excited I can barely breathe. And when she finally comes onstage at the end of the evening and says that she'd rather read a poem than make an acceptance speech, I know in my gut that my prayers have been answered and the poem she'll read will be this favorite one of mine. And as she begins to speak the lines I know by heart—*A dark woman, head bent, listening for something*—I think to myself, *this* is one of those moments. To be sitting here at the elbow of my dear friend, and also at the feet of this clear-sighted woman, bathing in the balm of these good and honest words. I throw a glance toward Jane to make sure she knows how this is for me, and before I've even asked the question with my eyes she nods.

These are not the roads / you knew me by, the poem concludes, *But the woman driving, walking, watching / for life and death, is the same.* At this moment, and for a little while after, there will be nothing else on earth I need.

Pregnancy and Other
Natural Disasters

I n February of 1997, I discovered I was pregnant. The timing, I thought, couldn't have been better. I was thirty-five years old. I had a home base, a loving partner, and my second book of fiction nearly ready to turn in. After almost twenty years of collecting passport stamps and bad relationships and a list of outdoor adventures so long it was getting hard to keep them separate in my memory, I believed I was ready to hang up my backcountry skis and my whitewater rafts and my whole collection of Lonely Planet Wilderness Travel Guides. I believed I was ready to excel at the mostly indoor sport of motherhood. I believed I was ready to grow up.

For the first few weeks of the pregnancy I was happy, or at least able to convince myself I was. But during the second month a depression settled in around me that by the third month had turned suicidal. My doctor said mood swings were common but I couldn't make him understand that I wasn't swinging. I was down in a hole so deep I couldn't get out of bed in the morning, and sometimes not even in the afternoon. I was in a place so dark that none of the things that usually heal me—the sight of the mountains outside my window, or Van Morrison's "Caravan," or even the stupid pet tricks of my Irish wolfhound—could make me glad to be alive.

Things will improve in the second trimester, my friends told me, but I couldn't even see how to make it through the day. I woke up each morning more and more sure that my life was over, that I had been handed a death sentence, and that even if I somehow lived through the pregnancy, the delivery, and the first few years of motherhood, my life would be devoid, for all that time, of everything I loved: grueling Himalayan treks, frigid winter camping trips, and the class 5 whitewater rivers that for so many years had energized and defined me. And as shallow and selfish as that might sound to anyone who has given up or greatly modified an active outdoor life to have children, the truth is that I didn't know how to exist without looking toward the next adventure. Those days and nights spent risking life and limb on the ocean, in the mountains, and down the rivers had been the things that let me know I was alive for as long as I could remember, and without them I didn't know who I was.

If those worries weren't enough to make me feel as unmotherly and superficial and generally awful about myself as I ever had, there was also the fear of watching my body change into something I could neither count on nor recognize. *Nine months up*, the books said, *nine months down*, possibly more for women over thirty, and though weight gain during pregnancy is hardly something a healthy person should hold against herself, I did, and in a big way. *A fat girl is nothing but a fat girl*, my mother used to say as she squeezed herself into her girdle every morning, *no matter what else she accomplishes in her life*.

Of all the misguided rules for living that my mother handed down to me, that is the one I think about most often, every time a bite of food leaves the fork and enters my mouth.

It wasn't just that my body was bigger than usual that scared me, but that it had become, almost overnight, completely useless as well. *Don't lift that*, is what I heard a hundred times a day from everyone around me, or *Don't push it*, every time I went out to hike or bike or ski. But I had always pushed it, and I didn't know how not to. I shoveled a few inches of snow out of my driveway at five weeks, bled all weekend and very nearly miscarried, and the doctor gave me such a lecture I was afraid to do anything after that. (I didn't even tell him that it was twenty-four inches of snow and that my driveway is a quarter mile long.) The challenge seemed to be to give up my strength and fitness for the better part of two years without drowning in self-hatred, and it was quickly becoming clear that I wasn't up to the task.

I understand now, half a year later, that much of what I was feeling in those early months of pregnancy was out of my control, a psychologically recognizable condition caused by a combination of hormones that soared and plummeted far more than they should have in what doctors call a "normal" pregnancy, and an entire childhood's worth of my own repressed memories that were fighting their way to the surface of my consciousness, trying to break through. I understand also that to say my fear of pregnancy was about having to give up outdoor adventures in remote locations is exactly the same as saying I love the jagged edges of danger—the rapids at high water, the back of a young horse in an open pasture when he's in turbodrive—because they make me feel excited and alive. Both statements are truths, but only partial ones. And the deeper truth behind them turns out to be the same.

I grew up in a house that was filled with anger and bitterness, so much rage that I was afraid nearly all of the time. The violence in my house was bred of resentment: my mother's resentment over sacrificing a promising acting career to get pregnant, my father's resentment over many things, including giving up his most-eligible-bachelor status to marry my mom. If we believe the theory—and I do—that we repeat our childhood traumas over and over as adults until we get them worked out, that is at least one explanation for why I keep finding myself in the middle of all those tornadoes and hypothermic 3:00 a.m.s and all those near misses with grizzly bears. It also explains why I was so afraid to give them up.

The only other time I was pregnant, my mother said, *You have a very special talent that sets you apart from most other women, and if you give it all up to have this baby you will become indistinguishable from every other woman on the face of the earth.* I didn't know exactly what she thought my talent was. If it was writing, surely having a baby wouldn't stop me from doing that. But the thing that seemed to set me apart from most people—even from most writers—is what I wrote about most often: trekking at sixteen thousand feet in Bhutan where I thought I'd had a heart attack, guiding a wild sheep hunt in Alaska that ended when a mud slide took our tents and supplies and almost our pack mules into the Sagavanirktok River, rafting down the Colorado during the highest water in a decade and flipping my raft in the rapid known as Satan's Gut.

Having a baby *would* have made it much harder to do those things, and if I didn't have those things to write about, would there have been anything else? I didn't know the answer, but the question terrified me enough to have an abortion, which I did in a clinic where I stared at a picture of a sailboat on the wall the whole time. Less than a year later, I was on a sailboat that looked just like it, fighting off Hurricane Gordon for two solid days in the middle of the Gulf Stream, ninety miles—but it might as well have been a thousand—off the Florida Coast.

What I realize now, several years after my mother's death, is that when she gave me her advice she had been talking not about me but about herself, and all that she had given up to have me. The abortion stands in the regret category of my memory, although when I add up the adventures, emotional and physical, I've had since then, they make a pretty good case for a decision that may have been arrived at poorly, but turned out, in the end, all right. And the reason I seek out adventures that come equipped with their own natural disasters turns out to be the same reason I was so afraid to have a baby. There is only one story of our lives and we tell it over and over again, in a thousand different disguises, whether we know it or not.

In late April, I had a miscarriage, and though part of my experience was sadness and loss, my overwhelming emotion was relief, like I had been given some kind of reprieve to figure out the answers to all the questions the pregnancy raised. Can I alter my definition of adventure to include sports that are several steps removed from real danger? Can I give my body eighteen months to be heavy and out of shape without dissolving in self-loathing and disgust? Will motherhood turn out to be an even more satisfying adventure than the ones I've had so far? Will I be able to work with my own childhood memories thoroughly enough to break the chain of violence and resentment that was so much a part of my past? Is it possible that in spite of (or because of) everything I've said here, the undeniable truth about me is that I can't now and will never be able to resist the sharp teeth of adventure?

What I can say with confidence is that I'm working on the answers, and will continue to, whether or not I decide to get pregnant again. In the meantime, I'm lining up a few more adventures. I'm going in December to ride with the gauchos in Patagonia. I'm thinking about another early-spring dogsledding trip on Alaska's North Slope. I hike in the mountains near my house every day, and try to come down before the afternoon lightning starts to crackle above me and raise the hair off the back of my neck, before it slams into the tundra only a few feet away from me and makes me run as if from God himself. I don't always make it below tree line before the real trouble starts, but I'm getting better at anticipating the oncoming storm. I hear it telling me in advance to take care and take cover, and more and more often these days I do.

Breaking
the Ice

I t's March 21, 1998, a day known to scientists and pagan
worshipers as the vernal equinox, the day the sun rises and
sets at zero degrees latitude along the earth's equator, or, more
precisely, the day the earth spins on its axis perfectly perpen-
dicular to the sun. Today the sun is above the flat horizon for
exactly twelve hours; tomorrow, it will be up there just a little
bit longer.

As a person who finds her faith in the consistency of the
patterns of the universe, and as an acute sufferer of seasonal
affective disorder (SAD), I consider this a big day. Maybe the
biggest. On December 21 I feel a measure of relief, because
even though I have most of the winter in front of me, I know
that the days, unbearably short as they are, will get a little
longer as each one goes by. On September 21 I feel nothing but
flat-out panic that we are about to enter the long slide into
darkness that feels like an annual survival test. People think
June 21 should be a seasonal-affected person's happiest day,
but it's really joy mixed with trepidation. June 21 may be the
beginning of summer, but each day will get a little shorter

from then on. March 21 is the only truly joyful day: twelve hours of daylight and nothing but clear sailing ahead.

In the winter I rise at first light and spend as many hours as the weather allows outside, taking advantage of every moment of light the stingy heavens offer. But soon there will be so much daylight I won't know what to do with it. I might sleep in every so often. I might even take a nap in the middle of the afternoon.

My friend Marilyn is visiting from Boston—a place with winters far darker than here—and we are celebrating the equinox together. What this has involved so far is walking each day the half mile to the creek that borders my property, hanging over the edge of the bridge, and throwing rocks at the ice until holes start to form. The weather has been changeable, which here means brilliant sunshine mixed with snow squalls so thick and sudden that you can't see your hand in front of your face.

What started out as the casual tossing of a few rocks over the edge has turned, over the course of the last five days, into something far more serious. Now we are hauling boulders the size of microwave ovens up onto the bridge. We are taking turns—one of us bracing herself against the bank and holding on to the other's arm while she ventures out on the ice and stamps its edges for all she is worth.

We have gone through several pairs of pants and shoes each, and with all the rocks we have moved this week we feel we may have seriously jeopardized the structural integrity of the bridge. None of these things seems important. We are on a mission. We are two women with seasonal affective disorder doing what we can to make spring come.

————

If anyone had told me five years ago, when my best girlfriend Sally died of breast cancer, that it would take me five years to let another woman this far into my life, I would have said they were insane. I knew Sally's death had rocked me hard, coming as it did only eight months after the sudden death of my mother and a few months before the end of my marriage.

When my mother died, my husband Mike said, "You don't really have to go into therapy about this because you have me to talk to." When Sally died he said, "Well, you knew she was going to die for so long that you've done all your grieving; you should be fine from now on." Poor as it was, I took his advice and avoided everything, a list that eventually included him and any potential women friends who might have come my way.

I made friends in those years with men, who didn't have breasts and seemed therefore immune to cancer. I had mammograms I didn't need, spent way too much money on health insurance, and waited for the inevitable diagnosis that would do me in. My mother had always said about my father, "He's so mean, he'll outlive both of us," and so far he's outlived her by six years. With my father well into his eighties, I believed that my mother's prophecy sealed the fate I already had imagined. It took me years to understand that not absolutely everything my mother said would come true.

I've never been very good at expressing what my mother used to call the "negative emotions": sadness, anger, frustration, fear. In the house I grew up in, my mother and I weren't allowed to have them. My father made up for our deficiency in the "negative emotions" by having them all the time.

In the last several years, it seems, I've grown into frustration, had a soirée or two with anger, have been working really hard getting fear into my repertoire, but sadness (a thing much different from depression) still eludes me.

If I had gone to therapy when Sally died, sadness might have been the first thing we worked on. Now, five years later, it's the last holdout, the voice in my head, my mother's or mine, still saying, *We must never admit to how sad we are; if we do we will die of grief.*

I suppose it is possible that if I had, as a child, let myself feel sad about the things that were happening to and around me, I might have laid down and died from it. But I'm thirty-six years old, a woman with my own life now, and never is too long not to have the experience of being sad. It's not coming easy to me, and I don't know which I fear more, who I am if it doesn't come, or what will happen to me if it does.

If a cancer patient shows a clean bill of health for five years she is considered cured in the language of statistics. I always thought that the five years was a random number, and I find it somewhat ironic that it seems to have worked for me too. Five years almost to the day after Sally died, I finally gave up the deathwatch I never should have embarked upon. I stopped with the yearly mammograms. I finally made a close friend.

Although we look so much alike that people take us for sisters, Marilyn's life is as different from mine as night from day, and though we grew up in households that were fraught with the same kinds of anger, Marilyn reacted to hers in an entirely different way. As practical as the Volvo station wagon she carts her kids around in, Marilyn decided at twenty-one that babies were better than grad school, and anything was better than home. She married the first really decent man who asked her and had three kids in a row, the first so severely handicapped that the doctors said he would die within a week; they recommended that Marilyn save herself the heartache and simply let him go.

But Marilyn had had a lot of experience with heartache already and she took her newborn home and sang Fleetwood Mac songs to him—"Landslide" and "Silver Spring"—every night, and did a lot of other things I can't begin to imagine. He's twenty now, beating the odds so many times the doctors have stopped saying anything at all. Her daughters are smart and beautiful and on their way to boarding school at Phillips Exeter. Listening to her talk to them on the phone has been one of the very few things that has made me wish I had kids.

Marilyn doesn't find it nearly as astonishing as I do that she has made a marriage work for more than twenty years. She knows with absolute certainty that if her husband were to leave her another man would want her. "It's got nothing to do with how we look or what we have to offer," she says, as though it's a foregone conclusion. "Women like you and me radiate light."

We met on the Cape, and now we spend a week together there each summer. Last fall she came to France with me, and now she's here in Colorado at the ranch. Though she and her husband live well, when I met her she'd scarcely been out of New England. Now I try to talk her into one trip after another—a weekend in New Orleans, a horseback trip in Ireland—and she just gives me a look that says I'm missing the point.

I know that she's a little afraid that when I visit her for the first time later this summer I'll see how domestic her life is and it will send me running. She's as wrong about this as I'm wrong when I try to entice her with faraway trips.

In spite of this, my friendship with Marilyn solidified in France. I had taken a group of women there for ten days of writing and touring. Marilyn was my right-hand woman, her rent-a-Fiat keeping up with my rent-a-Citroën on the tight turns and corners, she and I going out at dawn for croissants and orange juice, she giving the steering lessons when we canoed down the Dordogne. We were one bed short in the rented farmhouse, so Marilyn and I shared the only queen.

We loved each other every minute of that trip, but neither of us is the type to venture too far out there with our feelings. We got into bed each night like a couple of truckers, both in our ankle-length flannels.

"Nice driving today," I'd say as I turned out the light, and she would say,

"Same to you."

I wasn't with Sally on the day she died. It was February 8, a time when the light is returning, but so slowly that March 21 seems longer away than it really is. I was on a book tour, moving from city to city so fast I could tell myself that the fact of not having heard from Sally in over a week was more a function of my schedule than any real cause for alarm. When I got home to Utah I found out that no one else had heard from her that week either.

Sally had left her home, her husband Ben, and her son Eli

in Utah over a month before to follow a doctor who had given her faith in a highly experimental protocol. She had been staying at a motel in Tulsa, Oklahoma, but when I pressured the receptionist at the motel she finally admitted that Sally had checked out over a week earlier, and as far as she knew had gone to the hospital. The hospital nurse on Sally's floor said she wasn't taking calls, and when I begged to talk to her roommate, she wouldn't tell me anything either. Finally a distant aunt of Sally's called me back in tears.

"I promised her I wouldn't tell anybody what was happening," she said, "but you have to come quick if you want to see her. It's a terrible thing," she said. "She's all blown up and yellow."

I called Ben and told him to pack a suitcase. Then I went to the ski area to find Eli and his snowboard on the slopes. At the airline counter the woman talked about bereavement fares and death certificates. "Oh, my mom's not going to die," Eli said, and that's when the concourse started spinning around me. Sally was the most honest and present person I had ever known, but the disease had taken even that away from her. She was hiding from all of us, and part of me understood that was her privilege; the rest of me just hurt for Ben, and more than that for Eli, and most of all for myself.

We were still at the gate in Salt Lake City when the page came through for Ben. The next few seconds were the least real part of it: the way Ben started crying first and then Eli, and then a man approached, only seconds later, as if from central casting, all in black.

"I'm a priest," he said. "Can I help?"

I didn't go with them. I stayed in Utah and watched their

dogs and their horses, and picked them up at the airport when they brought her ashes home. I drove home from the airport alone that day into an early-February twilight and then listened to my husband say how good it was that I wouldn't have to grieve. I didn't cry, then or at the funeral. What settled in me instead of grief was a slow and steady anger, and a wall that took five full years to come down.

I've written about Sally several times since she died, in both fiction and essays, but I'd never even tried to write that airport scene. As I begin to work on this essay, I will tell my therapist about finally getting to the airport scene and he will ask why I think it took me so long to write it.

I will talk about how writing changes an event forever. No matter how much I may try to record it accurately, once it is written it is subject to the alterations I have made, whether they are slight or major, and I can never trust my memory 100 percent after that. I will tell him that there are certain things about Sally that I haven't wanted to let go of, how I haven't wanted to let even something as personal as my writing interfere with my memory of certain events.

"What things about Sally were you trying to preserve in that way?" he will ask.

And of course it will be therapy, so my mind will race around like it always does trying to get the right answer. Surely the day at the airport can't be it, I will think, that day of negligence and bad timing and final and irreparable loss. Surely there are good things, happy things, I want to preserve too, days before and even after she got sick when we were close and laughing and as in love as two heterosexual women can be. But hard as I will try to find a positive thought, my mind will just keep coming back to the scene at the airport.

"It's strange," I will say tentatively, "but it seems like I have been trying to save that airport scene more than any other."

My therapist will get the stifled smile on his face that he reserves for moments just before a major breakthrough.

"And why do you think that would be?" he will say.

And then the truth will wash over me and I will sit in his office and I won't be able to stop grinning. "Because there is value in the sadness," I will say, and his smile will be really uncontainable now. "It can fill you up," I will say, and I will mean it, "like happiness can, only in a different way."

We will sit quietly, then, both of us watching the wheels in my head turn.

"It's just part of being alive," I will say, rolling now, saying things every healthy five-year-old knows and feeling wise beyond my years at the same time. "And if sadness really doesn't kill you," I will say, "then you're home free in every situation, then no emotional risk is too great."

Half the things on my worry Rolodex will be vanishing like thought bubbles. Maybe more than half. I will feel like I might levitate off the couch and start floating around the room.

"This might be a good place to stop for the day," he'll say, and I'll smile back at him.

"Good idea," I'll say, "we're sure not going to do any better than this."

We spent the first few days of Marilyn's visit in Denver staying at the historic Oxford Hotel. I had big plans for us: massages, fancy dinners, clothes shopping, and pedicures.

Marilyn was very clear, however, that she didn't want anyone to touch her body, and what we wound up doing was walking around the city park talking until we were exhausted and then coming back to the Oxford for room service and a Fleetwood Mac concert on PBS.

We've been at the ranch five days now, and the days have taken on a rhythm of their own. We read in the morning, and if something occurs to us, we write a little. We march down the road to the creek like soldiers on a mission. We spend the heat of the day there throwing rocks, discussing fracture lines and strategies, getting soaked. We walk home satisfied, take turns in the claw-footed bathtub, cook something fresh and delicious to eat.

The strangest part of all this is that we've almost stopped speaking. It's not because we are mad, or even because we've run out of things to say to each other. It's something far better than that.

It's as though the snowmelt and the lengthening days have simply taken hold of us. As though we have tacitly agreed to accept the silence the mountains demand in this silent season. Summer is the time for talking, the mountains say, when the birds are singing and the creek is gurgling and there are leaves on the trees that will rustle in the wind. Now is the time to sit silently together, to feel the ice break around you, to wait for the first bluebirds to return to the feeder; now is the time to heal.

Tomorrow the visit will be over and I will take Marilyn to the airport. We will leave the house at 4:00 a.m. and will sing to the tape I made (Girl Songs, '98) most of the way. David, my wonderfully sensitive boyfriend, who will have been sleeping in the backseat most of the way, will wake up just in time to try to get us to *share*.

As we turn onto the ten-mile, airport-accessing Frederico Pena Boulevard I will lower the stereo, and David will ask why and I'll say, "In case any of us needs to make any closing remarks."

"Oh, like what," he'll say, "like you might want to say how happy you are that your friend came to visit you?"

I will think about what a beautiful thing the silence was between us. I will think of how it was the first time since Sally's death that I let ten days go by without doing any work.

"Yes," I will say, eyes fixed on a Pinto full of Rastafarians in front of me, "in case we want to say anything like that."

"It was a great week," Marilyn will say quietly, and I'll agree, but that won't be enough for David.

"The two of you," he'll say, "two women who love each other so much and are still afraid to express their feelings."

I'll giggle uncomfortably, and Marilyn, who will be red to her ears, will turn full around to face him and say, "Look, David . . . we're *fine*."

It is a moment I will remember for its perfection. Two of the people I love most in the world being perfectly themselves.

And Marilyn will be right. We are fine. Whatever we say or don't say at the airport.

We've just spent seven days making spring come. From this day forward, the days will be longer than short.

Dispatches
from
five
continents

———————————

African
Nights

I went to Africa to look for the animals. Not the exotic or rare ones, necessarily—the vanishing white rhino, or the shy swamp-dwelling sitatunga—but the animals of my childhood story books, the ones my safari-guide husband said would be easy to find: elephants, lions, zebras, giraffes. Africa, I knew from the newspapers, was in crisis, her people desperate and lost, but I hoped I could look beyond the poverty and politics long enough to see the wild country I knew was disappearing, a part of the world so unique and precious that it couldn't possibly survive the hostilities around it for long. I wanted to feel the rhythms of the dark untamed heart of Africa before they disappeared forever. I wanted to hear the wild night cries of the animals. I wanted them to show me the steps to their ancient and unfamiliar dance.

I went to Africa with my husband, Michael, who grew up there, who spent the three years before I met him working as a guide in Botswana, taking groups of tourists into the country he would now share with me. We brought along two American friends, Christine and Suzanne, and Michael's Tswana friend and assistant guide whose name was Better—or rather, Better was what he called himself because, he said, we had no hope of pronouncing his real name.

Our starting point was Maun, the city on the edge of the Okavango Delta that supports Botswana's safari industry, twenty thousand Tswana (and exploding), and about five hundred white expatriates—safari guides, pilots, writers, biologists—from one first-world country or another.

In some ways, the white community in Maun is not unlike one you would find in any isolated tourist town in America— Telluride, Colorado, say, or Key West. Maun's white population are for the most part intelligent, interesting, incestuous, and gossiping people; they have a lot of disdain for mainstream living; and a lot of them do way too many drugs. They have neither the creative generosity nor the humanitarian resilience of the Africans (who, I discovered instantly, were neither lost nor desperate), and for that reason, as well as others, they don't mix with the black Africans socially, even in a place where there is as little else to do as there is in Maun.

There are three bars in Maun that cater to white locals, and the first night we were there we went to a Lions Club dinner at the Duck Inn, where the only blacks in attendance were the ones serving the food. The woman who owns the Duck Inn is named, improbably, Bernadette Peters, but most people just refer to her as Ma Duck. She is tough and fearless, and with good reason. One of the many colorful rituals that take place in the small hours of the morning at the Duck Inn is a penismeasuring contest where all the men who are left standing drop their pants and squat on the bar while the least inebriated woman records the lengths.

Maun is a town full of hunters and safari guides, a painfully familiar breed of white man that, even by cowboy standards, takes "macho" to some new incalculable extreme. These men are polite, capable, and so delicately superior that it is almost possible to mistake their condescension to women for protectiveness or responsibility. They will never, not one of them, look a woman straight in the eye.

"Every woman who comes on safaris," I was told four times during the Lions Club dinner by three different tall, broad, and slightly Aryan guides, "expects to sleep with the guide at least one night before she goes home."

"No question about it," Heinrich, from Frankfurt, told me over dinner, his eyes flicking from my cheek to my collarbone, "they think it comes with the price of the package." (I knew as he said it that I, of course, would be sleeping with the guide on our trip, because he was my husband, and also because, thankfully, he was mostly past the "safari-guide stage" in his development when I met him. Christine, Suzanne, and I began referring to his temporary regressions into prerelationship behavior as the Dr. Jekyll/Mr. Guide syndrome.)

Not really welcomed, not really driven to leave, Maun's mostly young expatriates cling to an idea of Africa, to a wild-country ethic that is fading faster than they can decide where to go next. Soon the road from South Africa to Maun will be paved. Soon the population will double again.

I have spent most of my adult life in towns where all people talk about is the way things used to be, and I was not sorry to leave Maun. As we rolled out of town in a borrowed 1948 Land Rover whose name was Misery, I was anxious to leave behind the cattle and the donkeys and the overgrazed land, the nervous tension between bored whites and hungry blacks in a city about to get big. As we bounced along the sandy two-track in the seating configuration that would become regimen (Mike driving, Better riding shotgun, women, always, in the back), I was hoping there was still one place in Africa that felt untouched, unburdened, and wild.

Ten miles out of Maun the roads became so deep and rutted they rattled my brain beyond clear memory. After the better part of a day (about forty miles), Misery chugged to a halt in a village called Ditshipi, where Better and Misery would wait for us while we went, by boat, four days deeper into the delta.

Ditshipi is one of many bushman villages in the Okavango Delta, home to a handful of craftsmen who make long, thin dugout canoes called *mokoros*. For thirty *pula* a day (U.S. $15—a good wage by Tswana standards) the bushmen use a thin gum-tree pole to push tourists and guides and all their gear up the Santatadibe River into the heart of the delta, the place where even the four-wheel-drive roads don't go.

Unlike Better, who lives in Maun, has a car and a TV, and sends his kids to a government school, the polers and their families live a life almost untouched by commerce, material-ism, and all of the good and evil that town life can bring. Tourism is the flaw in the system: we bring them the money they didn't need before we came.

Mike was hoping we'd find his favorite poler in Ditshipi, a man who calls himself John White, but the villagers told us that John White was out making a mokoro. Every year or so, the men in the village disappear into the bush, go through an ardu-ous tree selection process, cut one down with a blunt ax, fashion their boat with the same tool, and then soak it, for weeks, just under the surface of the delta water. When they return to the village, to their wives and families, it is with a new mokoro . . . most of the time. I did not immediately understand that "making a mokoro" could also be a metaphor; it was the way the husband told his wife he'd be spending a little time away. Consequently, it is the bushwomen who organize the society, if not in theory, at least in practice, and as a result the women are hardworking, reliable, straight-backed, beautiful, and patient as stone.

Our polers' names were Robert, Master, and John. For the four days we would be with them they would carry our bags, build our fires, and keep us away from the hippos, who had been known to bite mokoros right in half. They would eat whatever we left in the pots for them, and then whatever we left on our plates. They would show us a tiny percentage of what they knew about the delta, and they would hate us, just a little, the whole time.

Robert was the leader, and the angriest. He understood English—his favorite expressions were "hallelujah" and "number one." He developed a crush on Christine and made her a necklace from a water lily. She looked like the princess of the Okavango as he poled her around a lagoon in his boat.

Master understood English, but he pretended not to; he was happier than Robert, and had a deep infectious laugh. He showed me, without speaking, which water plants had edible roots, how to make wine out of palm leaves, and where to look in the acacia tree to find honey so sweet and pure it was like nothing I've ever tasted.

John knew the most about tracking animals, the least about white people. He was very young, but very good with his mokoro. He made us each a musical instrument called a swohorohoro, from some bits of gum tree and a reed, and tried to teach us how to play.

Watching the polers and Mike interact, in their distinctively Faulknerian love/hate dance, was a little disconcerting. I know that my husband is not a racist, but after seeing the house in South Africa he grew up in, after seeing Johannesburg itself with its millions of white suburban homes, each one walled up neatly and plastered with Armed Response warning signs, after meeting the professorial black man named Peter Mmutle who helped raise Michael, and who was, in fact, the king of the northern division of the Sotho tribe—over a half a million people—and who still, in fact, lives in a Sears "Tuff-shed" in Michael's sister's walled-up backyard, I realized that Mike and I came from places more different than I had imagined, and I watched him, more closely than I ever had before.

"I think Robert likes you," I said to Michael, which seemed to me both true and impossible.

"He doesn't like me," Michael said, in an even voice that presumed no power. "He thinks I'm God."

Around the rest of us, the polers were quiet and reserved, but as soon as they decided we weren't paying any attention they turned back into the boys they were, racing their mokoros, talking back to the baboons that surrounded our camp, climbing trees themselves to find comfortable seats, silhouetted against a raging red African sunset, laughing and teasing each other in their uninscribable bushman tongue.

On the second day in the delta we saw our first elephants. We were in the mokoros, heading upriver, when suddenly there was a lot of incomprehensible and excited whispering from the polers. Two great gray bodies thrashed in midriver less than fifty yards in front of our boats.

"Are they fighting?" I whispered to Mike.

"No, they're playing," he whispered back. And sure enough, the elephants were playing, the way we would see, before our trip was over, a hundred pairs of elephants play. They rolled over and around each other, engaged in a dance that was both rhythmic and graceful, in spite of their size and shape. They took up gallons of water into their trunks and sprayed themselves and each other, rolled upside down into the river until all that was showing was their feet. They banged their heads together and flapped their ears over each other's faces and dunked each other using their heads and shoulders, or even occasionally their front feet.

As our polers inched us closer to them we could see that Mike was right; there was nothing but playfulness between them, no anger or dominating aggression. If there was anything besides play in the water dance it would have to be called joy, or love.

The polers got impatient with the elephants; it was getting close to sunset, and sunset is hippopotamus time. We were less than twenty yards away from them, but still well beyond their range of vision, and there was no way to pass safely by. Robert rapped sharply four times with his pole against the mokoro to get their attention. The elephants looked first in our direction, and then at each other, and then, more disappointed than angry or frightened, they stood up and jogged across the river and away from us, kicking massive arcs of water between us and the setting sun.

The rhythm of the delta infected us; we woke at first light, walked the game trails in the morning, and took long naps in the heat of the day. We traveled by mokoro in the afternoon and cooked our dinner over an open fire with increasingly older meat and vegetables (which were already a week old when we bought them in Maun). The most important thing we did all day soon became checking off our list of the animals we'd been able to approach, either by foot or by water, sometime during the day: zebra, lechwe, wildebeest; saddle-billed stork, warthog, wattled crane. We saw more elephants every day: running, swimming, playing, making giant mud holes in which to roll. Our initial fear gone, we'd let them walk within a few feet of us, their nearsightedness and the wind direction keeping us safe. When we were close to the elephants we heard the throaty rumblings of communication between them, heard the dry leaves of the lala palms rattle like maracas as they laid their trunks against them, knocking down the ripening seeds, and we heard them bellowing to each other at all hours of the day and night, surrounding and ignoring us, like the tiny things we were.

The dust of the delta sank into our skin, giving us a strangely gray/brown indeterminate color. That dust got in our ears and under our nails and so deep into our pores that no amount of brief hippo-wary swims in the Santantadibe would get it out. When we finally left the delta, when the mokoros rounded the last bend on the river and we saw Better and Misery waiting for us on the bank, Better asked Mike in Tswana what had happened to the white people he'd dropped off only a few days before.

We had a lot of driving ahead of us, two days worth (150

miles), until we got to the next game area: Moremi Wildlife Reserve. We drank warm tonic water (malaria protection) out of aluminum cans, read from our guidebooks, and took some time to observe and understand the ritual greeting dance of safari guides. When two trucks full of tourists pass each other (this can happen anywhere from two to ten times a day), the two guides grind their respective gears to a halt, hop out of their trucks, and meet in the middle of the sandy road, feet apart, hands behind their backs, khaki shirts rippling in the light afternoon breeze. What they talk about, while all the tourists sit roasting inside the hot truck, is anybody's guess.

"Mundane stuff," Mike assured me. "Sand pits, mud holes, weakened bridges, and the like." After two long days and way too many of these updates, we arrived safely at Moremi Wildlife Reserve. The big difference between visiting the parks in Africa and visiting the parks in America is that in Africa you can't get out of your car and go for a hike. The other difference is the reason: there are many more things in Africa that will eat you alive.

The advantage of the no-hiking rule is that the animals have grown to accept vehicles and not be threatened by them. For better or worse you can drive within a few feet of a lion and her cubs on a buffalo kill, a few feet of a leopard dozing in a tree, a few feet of a lagoon full of hippopotamus. If what you really want to do is get close to the animals, you'll never get closer than you will in a four-wheel-drive vehicle. The drawback of the rule is obvious: the experience is a little bit like going to a bigger, wilder version of Lion Country Safari. And while I loved being eyeball to eyeball with a satiated lioness, wouldn't I have loved it more if I had to crawl on my belly across hot desert sand? Wouldn't I have been a little more excited if there was just the remotest chance that she might suddenly leap up and eat me?

Thankfully, for those of us who need to at least imagine we are in danger to have a good time, there's a rule in the parks that forbids any driving between sunset and dawn. I believe it is this rule (though controversial and subject to change) that keeps the bush partially wild. In the daylight, Africa belongs to the tourists; after dark, the animals reclaim the bush.

We spent our nights sleeping on top of Misery under all those unfamiliar Southern Hemisphere stars. We went to bed not long after dark each night, and I would lie awake and wait for things to happen. First the night sounds would begin: the crickets and toads, the hyenas and their electronic-sounding *wwhhoooop, wwhhoooop*, the giant eagle owl's *woo-hooo, woo-hooo*, the baboon's sudden screech and constant chatter, an elephant's occasional angry trumpet, and finally, deeper into the night, the moan of an approaching lion. I would lie there, awake and unmoving in the dark, while a vervet monkey jumped into our truck looking for oranges, while two hyenas fought in the dying light of our campfire, giggling more maniacally than any human being. I'd fight sleep as long as I could, not so much because I was frightened (although I was) but because I was afraid of what I would miss.

Later in the night I'd wake to large dark shapes moving just beyond the trees that surrounded our campsite, a convoy of hippos moving out of the river and into the veldt, where they would graze till just before dawn. Hours later Mike would touch my arm and whisper, "Don't move," and a whole pride of lion would be moving through the campsite, padding softly beside the truck, following the river and the buffalo, completely undistracted by vehicles and tents and smells of human beings. Another period of dozing and the franklins would start shrieking, the baboons would be back in camp for breakfast, the light would just begin to show on the eastern horizon, and the southern end of the Milky Way would ever so slightly begin to fade. Then it would be up and into the truck and out into the park's fifteen hundred square kilometers, in hopes of a glimpse of some animal we hadn't yet seen, some animal who in all likelihood had spent most of the dark night right under our noses.

One morning we were lucky enough to come upon a pack of African wild dogs, eight young adults and a whole pile of puppies. Long-legged, big-eared, brindle-colored, and weighing less than an average Border collie, wild dogs are smart, playful, and better at peaceful, communal living than any of their African (or American) human counterparts. Misunderstood and persecuted to a degree even more astonishing than the American wolf, remaining wild dog populations are few and far between in Africa, and shrinking fast. I'd been told about the wild dogs' organized hunting, how a bystander can watch them communicate, how they'll assign positions and give each other signals, how after the kill there will be no fighting or squabbling, how each dog will beg for and receive food from another.

The dogs we saw were hunting waterbuck: fat, fuzzy antelope with white bull's-eyes on their butts, at least four times the wild dogs' size and weight. The dogs barked commands to each other, lining up along the riverbank, the female dog yipping at the puppies to stay. One by one the adults started moving, jumping in and out of the small river soundlessly, light on their feet, closing in. The waterbuck were nervous, realizing they'd been surrounded. They picked a direction and made a run for it, there was a brief hysterical scattering of hoofs and pads, and much to the surprise of us and the dogs, every waterbuck got away.

We looked to see what had happened to the dogs' hunting plan and noticed that one young dog hadn't made it across the river. He was running up and down the bank on our side now, the last to cross. Four or five times he ran up and down the same half mile of bank, while the others watched silently from the other side.

"He's crocodile bait now," Mike said, "and he knows it. The longer he waits, the worse it will be."

The commotion of the hunt would draw the crocodiles to the area, and even though the dog only had to make one splash in the water, that one splash could turn him into the crocodile's lunch. Up and down the dog ran whimpering to his companions, who finally, it seemed, forgave him for ruining the hunt, and came down to the narrowest crossing place, crouched down, heads on forepaws, and yipped encouragement to him. Happy to be forgiven, and encouraged by his buddies, the little dog made two running starts and then jumped in and out of the river so quickly it seemed that he bounced off the surface of the water. A cheer went up from the three vehicles that had gathered to watch the mini-drama.

"Watch them reunite," Mike said, and we did. Every member of the pack came to greet the young dog, sniffing and licking and making soft gurgling noises, such a glorious welcoming for a failed hunter who had been only a short time away. The puppies jumped in the air and danced circles around the feet of the returned hunter, and he in turn danced around the feet of the older, more experienced dogs who had helped him. No kill had been made, there was no food with which to celebrate, but the dogs danced for joy at being safe and together, and we watched them trot happily back into the tall dry grasses, their feet seeming not to touch the ground.

The river Kwai is the northern boundary of Moremi, the town of Kwai just on the other side. We walked across the bridge one day to buy beads and baskets from the women who congregate on a dusty gray terrace outside of their mud and Coke-can huts, and weave and sew and sing and laugh. These are women whose sadness is written in deep lines in their faces and whose joy overflows out of them, spills over even to camera-carrying white tourists who want to pay them the next to nothing they ask for their beads.

"My grandmother says you can take her picture, if you want to," a little girl of nine or ten in a pretty blue dress said to me, indicating a woman of about forty, who was sitting and weaving light and dark strands of reed together to make a basket's rim.

When I took the grandmother's picture, she wouldn't smile, but now when I look at it I see that her eyes are warm, and she's holding the beginning of her basket forward, like an offering. "Now I go home with you, ma," she said, and I knew in that instant she was right, and I wondered what kind of place she imagined when she looked at me and said that word "home."

From Moremi we went to Chobe National Park for more animal-rich days and cool, raucous nights. Our checklists got longer and more impressive: leopard, sable, pale-chanting goshawk, roan, lilac-breasted roller, eland, ostrich, corey bustard, steenbok, krake, African wildcat, oryx, reedbuck, puku, kudu, phuduhudu. Better tried valiantly to teach us the Tswana names—giraffe, *thutlwa*; hippo, *kubu*; baboon, *tshwene*; wild dog, *letlhalerwa*—and we tried as hard as we could to bend our mouths around the unfamiliar combinations of letters. By the end of fourteen days we had seen every animal we had a name for save one: only cheetah (in Tswana, *lengau*) refused to show his face.

Our safari had taken us slowly northward from Maun to the even smaller town of Kasane, but after so many days of nothing but sun, sand, and animals, civilization, even in a limited capacity, came as more of a shock than we imagined. All of a sudden there were bathtubs, running water, beds, lights, a bar with a sign that said, unbelievably, "Live music tonight."

We got clean, but only clean in a relative sense. What we had said about the dirt being ground in for life was not altogether wrong. We were 90 percent cleaner than we had been before we showered, which was at least 90 percent dirtier than we were used to being in our daily lives.

So as not to shock our systems entirely by being waited on in a restaurant (there was one in town) and to use up some of the food we overbought and would eventually give away, we drove Misery down to the town campsite for one last cooked-out meal: fresh (read: killed while we watched) chicken, gem squash, relatively fresh salad (it takes lettuce just five days to get to Kasane), and all the instant mashed potatoes I could find in the truck.

Before we finished dinner we heard the bar music begin, a not altogether bad imitation of Paul Simon doing "You Can

Call Me Al." We cleaned up the dishes quickly, with the luxury of tap water, and walked toward the music.

Unlike Maun's Duck Inn, this bar was full of every possible age, type, and color of person, and I had my first real glimpse of the kaleidoscope that Africa is made of, the African community that those twelve-foot walls try, and fail, to deny.

There was an East Indian safari guide, who had learned the chest-forward stance of his more common, blonder counterparts. There were the ex-owners of the bar, hunting brothers who looked so much like oompa-loompas from *Willy Wonka and the Chocolate Factory* that I can't remember their real names. There was a pack of Europeans, mostly young women in T-shirts and sandals, from one of the huge overland trucks that drive people from one end of the African continent to the other in thirty-eight days. There was a group of older black men, playing cards and keeping a low profile in the corner. There was a Jewish man from America who went to school in Salt Lake City, and wanted to talk to me about Mormons, nuclear testing, and AIDS. There were two British couples, dressed to kill in khakis and argyle knee socks, who were staying at the much more elegant Chobe Game Lodge (of Liz Taylor and Richard Burton fame) and who had come over to the Chobe Safari Lodge to see how the other half lives. There were two Tswana boys, drunk and having too much fun already, and an enormous Tswana bouncer who had his eyes on them hard.

But the people who were attracting the most attention were two beautiful Tswana women, by far the best-dressed, by far the best dancers, who entwined their arms and spun their skirts to every song that Danny, the soft-voiced musician from Cape Town, played.

A lot of alcohol got consumed that night, a lot of songs we thought we never wanted to hear again got played. From "American Pie" to "Sometimes When We Touch," from "Sweet Baby James" to "I'm Proud to be an Okie from Muskogee," through three versions of Eddy Grant's anti-apartheid song "Gimmie Hope Jo'anna [Johannesburg]," nobody went home early, and nobody sat down longer than it took to catch their breath. Danny said this was his last song seventeen times in the course of the night, and every time the hat got passed around to keep him playing everybody found something to throw in.

The young Germans did a sort of modified slam dance, the young black men, managing not to get kicked out all evening, did a slow reggae roll to whatever music played, the argyles cha-cha-ed, the Afrikaner oompa-loompa brothers did their childhood sakkie-sakkie, and the two beautiful black women made all of us look clumsy and danced all night without stopping, to the inner music of their bodies, their spirits connected to some other, more playful god.

And when it was finally over, when we walked back breathless and full of this late, unexpected taste of the real Africa, Christine took a step off the sidewalk and right into the back of a hippo, who'd come out of the Chobe River to eat the sweet green grass on the lawn of the Chobe Lodge.

"That's Esmerelda," manager Pat Tugwell called out her bedroom window. "We have a deal. She won't eat you if you give her plenty of room."

And Christine and I shrieked and giggled, and refused to acknowledge the danger that could have come upon us. We had the rhythms of Africa inside us. We were finally learning to dance.

Waves Every Color
of Harvest

I should have known all along that I would fall in love with the Ardèche, with the green craggy hills and the amber winelands, with the crystal laughing rivers that bubble and spill through the hand-hewn, tile-roofed villages, with the frank and hearty citizens of this little-known region of France that is mostly out of time and a long drive from anywhere and always at the mercy of the weather. I should have known I would fall in love if for no other reason than that it was September, and there's no way to keep myself from loving a place where I get to witness the deep and momentary sweetness of a summer's end.

Nestled between the region of Loire to the north and Provence to the south, between the banks of the Rhône to the east and the Cévennes mountain range to the west, the Ardèche is among the least talked about, least expensive, and least touristed regions of France. It is a place which at first glance seems without superlatives, a land of moderately high mountains and somewhat deep gorges, of medium-sized villages full of basically friendly people who produce reasonably good wine, and goat cheese and sausage so fat and salty you can feel the years slip off your life as you chew. It is a land of endlessly receding valleys full of goats and cows and an occasional farmhouse, and roads built by people who think driving should be a full-body workout, people who never mean you to get out of third gear.

Although the mountains and high villages in the Ardèche draw the eye skyward, it is in fact the rivers that dominate the landscape, that shape the land and the lives of the people who live there, that dictate where the Frenchmen build their wildly curving roads. The green Ardèche rises in limestone, the slightly bluer Eyrieux in granite, the mighty Loire in volcanic basalt. And each of these major rivers has ten smaller rivers that feed it, and five more streams that feed each of those ten.

The Ardèche may seem without superlatives, but only until the sun comes out on those river valleys, when it lights the orange roofs and the green fields glisten between rows of clean white stone, and you realize that you are as close as you have ever been to discovering some authentic unpretentious heart of France. For the Ardèche is the place the French go when they want to get back to nature, when they want to leave behind the bookstores and coffeehouses and spend a day in a kayak floating through unspeakably beautiful canyons, when they want to put packs on their backs and walk three days' worth of rugged mountain terrain.

My visit to the Ardèche begins in the town of Vals-les-Bains, located in the approximate geographic center of the region. I choose to shed my jet lag at the Hôtel de Europe, which is simple and clean and moderately priced, and the proprietors, Renée and Albert Mazet, couldn't be any friendlier, or more helpful to an unaccompanied female tourist speaking sleepy and halting French.

The town is lively, especially on market day (Saturday), when the streets close to traffic and vendors set up stalls containing all the local wares, from fruits and vegetables to an infinite variety of local sausage, cheeses, handwoven scarves, cassette tapes, honey, fruit juice, jeans, and grapes of every color.

Vals-les-Bains makes a kind of Mason-Dixon line in the Ardèche, marking the place where the region divides itself geographically, climatically, philosophically, and spiritually in half. To the north the winding rivers cut narrow valleys, and towns are roughly hewn out of the steep dark walls. The threat of winter is ever-present in the north country, the ridgetop winds sharp and unforgiving. Catholic churches dominate each village, and crucifixes, each one depicting a more agonized Jesus than the next, dot the sides of the hills.

In the southern Ardèche there are no crucifixes, and you can't find the churches (which are Protestant) for all the vineyards and cafés. From Vals-les-Bains the land rolls out to the south in waves every color of harvest, chubby farmers slow traffic almost to a stop with their tractor carts full of grapes, the smell of olive oil and garlic hangs as heavy in the village air as religion; in the late-afternoon sun, winter feels a lifetime away.

Because wine and garlic appeal to me more than damnation and sudden snowstorms, I decide to explore the southern villages first: Les Vans, Joyeuse, Aiguèze, all centuries old and poised somewhere between haphazard restoration and the simple luxuriousness of decay. There is a quiet beauty in these villages that is startling to my American eye: a single window box full of all-red flowers, the creamy tan of a windowsill against the blond stone of the walls, a row of purple weeds with a clothesline hanging in front of it, each piece of laundry either black or white.

The sign on the way into the village of Largentière says "1,000 years of history," and a white-haired woman walking her albino Afghan at the town's entrance looks like she's old enough to have seen all thousand years. As in every Ardechois town, a clear cold river tumbles through Largentière's center, giving it an energy, a vitality, that the quiet streets, too narrow in some places for even one vehicle, belie.

In spite of Largentière's age and sleepiness, I get the feeling that behind these walls lurk young people: it's the black dog with the red bandanna, the pair of psychedelic tights hanging on a line. Sure enough, I round a narrow corner and hear Van Morrison coming out of an open but gated window, and when I try to sneak a look inside, a thirty-something Frenchman with crazy black hair and a single dreadlock hands me a stem of purple grapes through the iron bars.

The major tourist destination in the southern half of the Ardèche is the Gorge of the Ardèche River, thousand-foot white walls of granite which rise out of the slabs of the vine-yard-covered countryside and wrap themselves around the riverbanks for a distance of approximately thirty miles. The narrow river road climbs sharply up the first granite fin and stays there, offering auto tourists only glimpses of the tiny green river far below, and leaving the gorge itself wild for the hundreds of hikers and kayakers that visit each year.

On the morning I arrive at the gorge there's a September nip to the air and a low clingy fog that makes the idea of sitting in a plastic boat just below waterline unappealing, so I reach for my hiking boots instead. The French build their trails much like they build their roads: a why-bother-with-switchbacks-when-it's-shorter-to-go-straight-up attitude that has its appeal, though it gives little long-term consideration to things like flash floods and erosion. Piles of debris—fallen trees, broken canoes, and lost water bottles—in the river bends tell me that in the springtime at least this quiet little river gets wild.

I climb to a point overlooking a deep meander, river bottom and cliff surrounding me on three sides. The early-morning mist is slowly lifting. A fish jumps a hundred feet below me, and near the side of the river water tumbles over a rock. Three kayakers paddle silently by; one opens his jacket as the river bends into sun. There are no rapids to speak of in the Gorge of the Ardèche, but there is enough current to give a beginning paddler a thrill, and the experienced river person a long lovely float down a mostly wild gorge.

The access town for the gorge is called Vallon-Point-d'Arc, which, after all the quiet, fifteenth-century villages I've been exploring, feels just a little like Gatlinburg, Tennessee. There are no quality hotels in Vallon-Point-d'Arc. Camping is available at countless places along the river, and you can rent anything you want there—mountain bikes, kayaks, canoes, fishing gear, horses—from any one of at least three dozen locations.

At a riverside café near Vallon-Point-d'Arc, a Frenchman in a battered paddling jacket takes considerable pains to explain to me that while the Gorge of the Ardèche River is thought of as the Grand Canyon of the Ardèche, the Gorge of Tarn in the neighboring province of Lozère is thought of as the Grand Canyon of all of France, and I shouldn't go home without seeing it.

Despite an approaching storm I take his advice, driving through the western reaches of the Ardèche, and climbing higher and higher into the ferny forests of the Cévennes. I pass through the mountain villages of Villefort and Point-de-Montvert and am tempted by the warm windowed cafés with backpacks and mountain bikes parked outside.

As the road leads out of Point-de-Montvert and winds along the river Tarn, still just a trout stream and falling fast, I get behind a Land Cruiser that can't seem to stay on its side of the road. The driver has his whole upper torso out the window and is leaning over, trying to see down into the gorge. The passenger's got one hand on the wheel, but he can't resist looking either. Every time another car comes along the narrow two-lane road, the blare of a horn and French curses force them into a deep swerve.

I recognize this instantly as internationally accepted river-rat behavior even before I note the two kayaks stuffed into the Land Cruiser's open back. The road bends away from the river, and I take that opportunity to pass. I give them the everything's okay sign in kayaker language (a simple two thumbs up) and they honk the horn and wave.

I turn away from the Tarn River onto a road that climbs even higher, around the side of Mont Lozère to a waterfall, Cascade de Runes. The west side of Mont Lozère was forested long ago, and what is left is golden terraces of field grasses, outcroppings of white stone, big-eyed dairy cows with bells around their necks, and endless fields of purple heather. It's hailing so hard now I'm starting to worry about how much insurance I took out on the rent-a-car, and then I pass a farmer who must be eighty with his black beret and his gold-tipped cane, taking his two hunting dogs for a walk.

Surrounding these farms and villages is the Parc Nationale des Cévennes, with limitless hiking opportunities. Brown signs point straight into the forest, or up toward a ridgeline, or between two stone fences marking fields. I choose the forest path and after just a few hundred yards I am surrounded by the softness and utter quiet of ferns and hemlocks. In three hours of walking the quiet is broken only twice, once by a German couple and their Border collie named Tasha, and once by a farmer and his donkey, looking for all the world like Cervantes, returning from his travels in the Cévennes. I wind back down toward the Tarn on a road that is little more than a farmer's two-track, and before long see the multicolored walls of sandstone and granite that form the Gorge of Tarn.

The fact is, neither the Gorge of Ardèche nor the Gorge of Tarn looks anything like the Grand Canyon, but I will admit to feeling a Grand Canyon–sized wonder as I stand on the edge of the Gorge of Tarn. I feel the heart-stopping astonishment that arises when the human eye gazes into more vertical space than it can at one time comprehend. The French have lent us a word for that final step beyond beauty . . . it is sublime, and Point Sublime is the best place from which to grasp the majesty of the Gorge of Tarn.

But here it is also possible to drive down into the gorge, to be suspended low, winding around the sides of the gray-streaked granite cliffs covered with weeping pines and hem-locks. There are stone houses built into the sides of these cliffs so old and permanent it is hard to tell where the cliffs end and the walls of the houses begin.

I stay that evening deep in the canyon at the Château la Caze, a fairy-tale castle beyond my wildest imagination, con-verted into a four-star *hôtellerie*. The rooms in the Château have names, not numbers, and the old woman in charge of things does not take too kindly to me arriving after dark and wearing sneakers, and alone. One pays for an opportunity to stay in a fairy tale not only with money (the Château was the most expensive place I stayed in the region), but also by sub-jecting oneself to the snootiness of Madame and her sidekick, the wartiest, mangiest German shepherd I have ever seen. But it is worth it to walk up the stone passageways worn smooth by five hundred years' worth of secrets, to throw open the doors on my turreted balcony and imagine armored suitors on the lawn, to climb into my canopy bed and wrap myself in lace older than I am, to pretend across cultures and centuries, to dream.

I stay, that night, in Anne's room, go to sleep remembering all of history's Annes and how many of them were doomed. I wake in the dead hours of the night with a fever that rages and makes my heart beat so hard I lie in the dark translating sentences of urgency. "How far to the nearest hospital? Can you call me an ambulance, please?"

The next morning my health is much improved, and I head back toward the Ardèche via the high road, which travels along the Corniche des Cévennes and affords a beautiful view of the entire Ardèche region. I stop my car at an overlook and walk out to a point. The altitude is nearly five thousand feet up here, and there's a bite in the air that carries more than a hint of the approaching winter. A handsome man in a tweed blazer carrying a bunch of heather in his arms meets me on the trail.

"*Bonjour, madame,*" he says. "*Il fait froid ici.*"

"*Oui,*" I say, "*il fait froid.*"

He smiles and walks on. When I return to my car there is a small bunch of heather stuck under my windshield wiper. This is what is so beguiling about the French: one minute they're disapproving of your sneakers, the next they offer you a bunch of grapes or a sprig of heather.

Back down in the Ardèche Valley the cold weather has brought on a flurry of activity. Farmers and their dogs are moving sheep down the hillsides, and the men pulling grapes with their tractors seem to have found an additional gear.

After spending the afternoon moving from wine cave to wine cave sampling what the Ardèche vineyards have to offer (some reasonable Cabernets and at least one excellent Merlot), I leave the wine country behind and climb, for what feels like hours, into the northern Ardèche, the town of Lamastre, and the Hôtel du Midi. By the time I arrive it is dark, foggy, and raining, and I'm tired, road-weary, ready to stay put for a few days and be taken care of. I am immediately charmed by the Hôtel du Midi, its bright window boxes and cheery yellow paint. I have heard the chef, Bernard Perrier, described as the region's best. But it is Bernard's wife, Marie-George, with her sly smile at my poor French, her instant warmth and generosity, who lets me know I've come to spend my last four days in France at precisely the right place.

"Have you an elevator?" I ask Pascal, one of the two hand-some waiter/bellboy/right-hand men that Bernard and Marie-George employ.

"No," he says, grinning, "you have me, and I am very strong."

"Very well then," I say. *"Allons."*

The room is elegant and rustic at once, furnished with antiques but sparsely and simply: a cherry-wood desk with curved legs, a hand-worked lace bedspread, a shiny brass lamp. The bathroom is bigger than any hotel room I've had so far, and in the center of it is the biggest bathtub I've ever seen. I am already in it in my mind when Pascal asks if I would like a table at eight o'clock.

"Eight-thirty, please," I say.

"Merci, tout à l'heure," he says, and then, in English, a heavy French accent with a faint California bite, says, "See ya later."

I am charmed beyond responding. It is the first English I've heard spoken in seven days.

Bernard Perrier's cuisine is quite simply the best I've had in my life. From the *amusé-bouche gourmand,* sautéed local mushrooms or a celery and salmon purée, to the traditional dish of the house, chicken baked in a pig's stomach, to a simple beef filet with artichokes, to the *soufflé glacé* that stands eight inches tall, there is nothing that comes out of Bernard Perrier's kitchen that is anything short of divine.

After the first evening I don't even look at the menu. Marie-George chooses my courses for me, Pascal suggests an appropriate wine. In four nights I will have sampled almost everything Bernard prepares, and I will have had it explained to me in detail by Marie-George, in a combination of French and sign language that includes buzzing her slender hands around her head to indicate honey, and making horns or floppy ears so that I understand the difference between beef and lamb. When I take my after-dinner walks she won't let me out the door without an umbrella. At breakfast she teaches me the French names of the flowers she's arranging for my room.

I spend four wonderful days in Marie-George's care. Each morning, after breakfast, I set out in a different direction into the wild countryside that surrounds Lamastre, and hike the endless trails that follow the ridgelines and the rivers, that connect the villages and the peaks. Bands of sunshine and clouds move through these mountains as quickly as urges; there is nearly always a rainbow somewhere in the sky. Most days the fog pours over the mountains as fast and as thick as running water. I get wet and cold and dirty gleefully, knowing that what awaits me at dusk is Bernard's lamb and Marie-George's feather pillows and an hour-long soak in my enormous tub. It is not lost on me that I am approaching some ultimate definition of the word *vacation*.

I decide on my last full day in the Ardèche to climb Mont Mézenc, the highest peak in the region. From its summit I can see first the hillside of sub-alpine firs stretching down to the terraced tablelands, the scattered villages of the Haute Vivarais—Chaudeyrolles the closest—and beyond that the gorges of the rivers, the Eysse, the Dorne, the Eyrieux, the bigger town of Saint-Agrève on the horizon. To the south the Cévennes stretch endlessly; I see Mont Lozère, where I was only a few days ago, forested hills and pastured valleys, a single stone farmhouse clinging here and there to a hillside catching the intermittent sun. Way out to the east I can see the edge

216 A LITTLE MORE ABOUT ME

of the high plateau, the empty space I know is the wineland of the Rhône; beyond the Rhône is another rise, the foothills of the Alps, and beyond that, I know, is Mont Blanc, standing almost three times higher than I am standing now, but the clouds have it surrounded and I can only see its base, a suggestion of where it might rise.

They say one goes to France to fall in love, and I did, first with Pascal's devilish wit, then with Bernard Perrier's exquisite food, and finally with Marie-George's kindness, a kindness that broke the language barrier between us without compromising her professionalism, and that made me feel more at home than perhaps I ever have abroad. By the time I had fallen in love with the Hôtel du Midi I had also fallen in love with Lamastre, the way it clings to the hillside around it like a sad and intelligent child.

Of course it was the land, above all, that I had fallen in love with. And as I climbed those craggy hills for the last time, past the dying vegetable gardens and herds of goats that had so quickly become familiar, a melancholy came over me way out of proportion for a ten-day holiday. And as I crested the hill that would take me out of Ardèche, down to the flatland and the highway, the airport, and eventually home, I realized that the leaves on the trees that covered the hillsides had all gone completely yellow, that in the time I'd been in the Ardèche, summer had turned into fall.

I pulled to the side of the road for a last look across the endless green valleys. Only when the sun went behind a cloud and the rain began again was I able to leave.

Soul of
the Andes

I am sitting with my friend Christine on the roof of a Toy-
ota Land Cruiser as it rattles down a rocky two-track in
Bolivia's tropical Yungas Valley. The Yungas Valley is a three-
hour drive and an entire topographical universe away from La
Paz, Bolivia's arid and treeless capital city. It is nighttime in
the jungle, and we hear rather than see the thousand-foot
waterfalls that tumble down the cliffs all around us, we feel
the spray as the Land Cruiser skirts them, we hear the night
sounds of the tropics, the wild music of colorful birds.

Between us is Marcelo Alarcón, our Bolivian guide, who is
charming, a little impish, multilingual to an astonishing
degree, and better dressed than any man either Christine or I
have ever dated. Marcelo is of mixed Aymara and Quechua
descent, the two tribes that make up more than 70 percent of
Bolivia's population. Our driver, Ramone, is *mestizo*—mixed-
blood, some unrecorded combination of the native people and
the *creolo*, the name given to European whites. Ramone is a
part-time singer in a mariachi band. He speaks Spanish,
Aymara, Quechua, and a little French. At the moment he is

singing in Italian, along with the tape: Pavarotti, and then Carreras.

Marcelo, Christine, and I pass a bottle of Cuervo Gold and a lemon between us. The stars are bright, closer here, I think, than I've ever seen them, though all the constellations are upside down.

"Is a lemon a thick-skinned fruit or a thin-skinned fruit, I wonder," Christine says. Our book has warned us not to eat, among other things, thin-skinned fruit.

Marcelo waves his hand dismissively. "In America, perhaps you need to pay attention to your book. In Bolivia, you need only to pay attention to the stars."

In this dark tropical sky, Regulus, the brightest star in the constellation Leo, turns from blue to red to white to blue again, and I can make out the shape of the Orion nebula with my naked eye.

"In America, when you worship," Marcelo says, bringing his palms together, "you hold your hands as though you believe you have the world inside them. When my people worship we open our hands to the world"—he spreads his arms wide, palms up—"like this."

This is our first trip to South America. We have chosen Bolivia because we've heard it is relatively safe and stable, because there it is still possible to encounter true Andean culture, because of all the countries in South America, it is the one our friends knew least about.

We wake through a slight tequila haze to the shrieking of a whole new set of jungle birds. Marcelo takes us to meet Patricio, a long-haired, bone-thin French expatriate who left Paris on an eight-day vacation seventeen years ago and never got around to using his return ticket. He raises coffee and bananas and Peruvian Paso horses on a hillside near the tiny Yungan town of Coroico, and runs a riding stable/café with his Vietnamese wife, Dani. They serve what is rumored to be the best cup of coffee in Bolivia, the buzz from one cup lasting two or three days.

Patricio, who is more manic even than his hot-blooded horses, takes us riding, fast and reckless, all over the jungled countryside, and then we go back to sit on his porch and talk about jungle politics, the DEA, and life in paradise.

"I sit on my porch bare-chested in the heat of the jungle," he says, "and all year long the mountains are white."

The view from his porch is almost too much to take in: banana palms and a chaos of bright purple flowers frame the Chario River below us. Beyond the river graceful green ridges write themselves across the landscape like Chinese script and shadow the valleys between them, which are deep and a slightly softer green. Above the farthest ridges, and shrouded intermittently by clouds, stand the dark volcanic rock and sparkling ice fields of the Cordillera Real.

"You Americans think you are free," he says, "but there are more animals than people in Bolivia. That is what I call freedom." A shadow crosses his face. "Now they are killing all the cougars. There are probably less than fifty spectacled bear." He slaps his forehead hard with his hand, momentarily Parisian. "I love the jungle," he says, "but all the time I am crying."

When we leave, Patricio gives us a bag of Dani's home-grown coffee beans. He says, "Remember, there are no doors on my house."

On the long dirt road that climbs out of the lush Yungas Valley, up and over the Cordillera Real and down onto the dry Altiplano, dogs stand sentinel like toll-takers hoping for scraps of bread and chicken. There is also a human stoplight, a man, Marcelo tells us, who lost his entire family in a crash on the blind corner where he now stands.

"He's been here every day for three years running," Marcelo says, "and says he will stand here the rest of his life."

We watch the man look both directions and lower the red flag, raise the green. Ramone rolls down the window to give him yesterday's *grenadillas* (passion fruit); he salutes the vehicle, and we go on our way.

When we cross the seventeen-thousand-foot-high La Cumbre Pass we leave the tropics as quickly as if they'd been a movie set and enter a landscape, lunar and a little surreal. Herds of llama wander across the barren Altiplano and the wind howls cold, though it is the middle of the South American summer. Angry clouds cling to the high mountain peaks, obscuring the summits. Mud huts are scattered across the countryside as randomly as stones from a rock fall. By the time we get to the outskirts of Bolivia's largest city, there is no vegetation at all.

La Paz, at 12,080 feet, is home to more than a million Bolivians. It is built in the bottom of a tortured, treeless canyon: the business district and the wealthy suburbs are in the very bottom of the bowl. The poorer you are in La Paz, the farther you live up the hill. The houses and huts that climb the hillsides are built on top of each other and the streets wander freely, unengineered, up the steep canyon walls.

Christine and I check into the Hotel Plaza, which is a model of first-world efficiency. It is located on the main thoroughfare called the Prado, walking distance from the markets and restaurants and the Plaza San Francisco, which is, with its history of bloodshed and drama, the agreed-upon center of town. From the Plaza's glassed-in Utama restaurant and bar on the eighteenth floor the city is spectacular. Night falls during dinner and we feel light-headed, suspended as we are inside the city: a giant bowl of sparkling lights.

The next day we climb the cobbled Sagarnaga Street above the Plaza San Francisco to the vast open markets, which are pure sensory overload: mountains of vegetables and huge hanging carcasses of beef and pigs; chickens, some roaming free and some dead and stinking; two hundred varieties of freeze-dried potatoes and spices by the hundreds of pounds. There are llama fetuses to bring good luck and stolen tape decks and watches; tiny sardines from Lake Titicaca frying in hot spicy oil; fizzy orange drinks with shriveled fruit in the bottom; at least ten kinds of chili paste; and fresh-baked meat-and-vegetable pies called *salteñas*. There are pan flutes, guitars, and small-stringed *charangos* made from the shells of armadillos; antique silver and ancient glass beads; hand-woven ponchos and colorful blankets; fresh-cut flowers and acres of coca leaves; and people everywhere, thousands of them, talking and hawking and yelling at once.

The merchants, who are predominantly Aymara and Quechua women, sit like colorful queens among their bags of goods. Their skirts, called *polleras*, are short and made of several bands of multicolored fabric, and their *ahuayos*, the bags they sling over their shoulders to carry groceries and babies, are brighter still. Their hair is braided into two long plaits and joined at the bottom by a tuft of wool called a *pocacha*, and on the top of their heads they wear, improbably but unfailingly, a dark green, brown, or black bowler hat.

Christine and I taste what we dare to taste: *salteñas*, *empanadas*, corn on the cob, chicken soup. We buy sweaters and socks and beads and charms that the witches insist will keep us healthy and bring romance. Exhausted by the altitude, and swooning from the smells of carrion and cayenne, we stumble back down the Prado to the plaza for some coca tea (believed to help altitude sickness) and a nap.

Early the next morning we're off to Chaclytaya, the world's highest ski resort, located ninety minutes from La Paz in the heart of the Cordillera Real. Christine and I dress in layers, unsure what skiing at 17,712 feet in the middle of summer will be like.

"Do you think the rental shop will take Visa?" Christine asks me, as we rattle up the cobblestones of suburban La Paz. The high mountains are in clouds again, and Marcelo mutters angrily about how we won't get a view.

An hour into our journey, just before the road narrows and really begins to climb, two Quechua men come running out of a hut, screaming at our car. Marcelo yells at Ramone to stop; he opens the door and the two men climb inside.

"These are the men who make the tea at the ski resort," Marcelo says. "If we want coca tea we have to give them a ride."

Christine and I exchange glances. "Probably the rental shop doesn't take Visa," I say.

The road narrows yet again, worsens, and is finally covered

with a layer of unmelted snow. The Land Cruiser spins its wheels, slides sideways and stalls, dangles, more than once, over the unprotected edge.

When we arrive at the "resort" our happy-to-be-alive adrenaline combines with altitude fever and makes it seem pure good humor that there is no lodge, no lift, no skiers, just a wooden shack and a three-inch steel cable that presumably, when it is running, serves as some kind of primitive tow line, though it makes my hands hurt even to look at it.

"No skiing today," Marcelo says, smiling. "Shall we climb the mountain instead?" Dizzy with altitude, we fail to realize how preposterous an idea this is.

Marcelo runs up the side of the mountain in his leather coat and Ray-Bans like a stylish little goat. Christine and I put one foot in front of the other, hearts pounding, shoulders aching, heads throbbing in the thin air as if our brains no longer fit properly into the confines of our skulls. The names of the surrounding peaks we can't see swim in my head, and I say them over and over like a mantra: Condoriri, Ancohuma, Huayna Potosí. We climb for over an hour and by the time we get to the top Marcelo has built us a snowman, and he is flinging snowballs into the void below.

"When I stand in these mountains and look toward the sea I think of my ancestors," he says. "These mountains"—he throws his arms up and out to take in the whole Cordillera Range—"are their gift to me. You must see the tops of them before you leave Bolivia," he says. "I will do what I can to lift the clouds."

That evening, back in La Paz, Marcelo takes us to Peña Naira for traditional food and music. We eat shredded beef with onions, tomatoes, and salsa that sits atop a mound of rice and reconstituted potatoes, and drink the frothy and light local beer called Paceña. Five fresh-faced boys sing as if their lives depend upon it and play instruments: guitars, *charangos*, pan flutes, rattles made of sheep's claws, a big rough-hewn drum. The panflute player blows his soft bangs up into the air with every puff of his lungs. He looks a little like Bono from U2 and I try to imagine him on MTV. Marcelo tells us all the songs are love songs, and when I ask him if the love is for a woman or for the land he says, "Surely you understand that this is the same thing."

The next day, we head across the Altiplano to Lake Titicaca, which, at 12,500 feet above sea level, is the world's highest navigable lake. On the way there Marcelo teaches us to say *How are you?* in Aymara, *Kamisaki*, and *Waliki*, which means *I'm good*. In the Bolivian summer there are thunderheads in the sky every afternoon, and we watch the massive anvil clouds build over the lake, which is crystal-clear and sapphire-blue. The lake stretches 150 miles northwest into Peru, but we take a hydrofoil only as far as the Island of the Sun, where we drink from all three spouts of an ancient fountain: the salty, the sweet, and the tasteless. Marcelo tells us this will guarantee us eternal youth.

The island's early inhabitants were members of the Tiahuanacan-Huari culture, a pre-Incan people who developed thriving religious, cultural, and political civilizations on the Bolivian Altiplano from 500 to 900 A.D. They believed the island was the sun's true birthplace and they built the intricate terraces that still cover every bit of land around the lake like a mad cartographer's grid. They built their temples at nearby

Tiahuanaco, and we go there to see them, to run our hands along the perfectly engineered walls hewn out of impossibly heavy stones brought in from inexplicable distances. We put our ears to a hole in the wall that allows a listener to hear the slightest whisper from a hundred yards away. We walk in a subterranean temple that has all the faces of humanity carved into its walls.

The next morning we leave Marcelo and fly south past the cloud-covered peaks of the grand Illimani, the 21,189-foot four-peaked mountain that stands watch over La Paz. We hoped the plane might get us above the clouds in time to see the rock and ice of Illimani's summit, but the pilot flies low and all we can see is the thick granite base of her, only a suggestion of her splendor reaching into the clouds.

A car meets our plane and takes us touring through the part of Bolivia known as the Valleys, red sandstone canyons cut by wide muddy rivers, our destination the mining city of Potosí.

"I am rich Potosí," ran the world's highest (13,349 feet) city's first motto, "the treasure of the world and the envy of kings." To this day most Potosíans swear by the city's mythology, that in 1544, when Diego Huallapa made his campfire so hot that molten silver started running out of the ground, there was enough silver in the mountain to build a silver bridge from Potosí to Barcelona, and still more silver to carry across.

In the two hundred years that followed that discovery, Potosí became the largest city in Latin America, an estimated eight million Africans and Indians dying from the horrendous working conditions in the mines. It is the real-life version of Conrad's *Nostromo*: a crumbling town that sits in front of a big hollow mountain. The silver ran out a hundred years ago, and the miners turned to extracting tin. When the price of tin dropped so low that even the government could only support a skeleton operation, the miners banded together and started cooperative mines, literally walking up to the mountain and digging their own holes. Christine and I stand in front of one of those holes now, a cooperative mine by the name of Santa Rita.

Juan Carlos Gonzalez is our guide for the day. He has taken us to a street market where we have bought presents for the miners: cigarettes, grain alcohol, coca leaves, raw sticks of dynamite, colored flags, and paper flower petals, offerings for the mine. The miners peer out at us from under bangs of thick black hair and felt hats. Their clothes and shoes are in tatters. Most of them will die from silicosis by the age of forty. In the best-case scenario they take home about eight dollars a month.

A woman stirs a pot of stew inside a mud hut near the mine entrance, and her children, all six of them, approach us sweetly, hoping for candy or gum. Juan Carlos gives us rubber jackets and hard hats. He mixes calcium carbonate and water in the cans of three antique lanterns and plays with the air vents until they hum and give off tiny flames.

"If the lanterns go out," he says in slow perfect Spanish, "make a run for it. It means there is no air left in the mine."

For Christine and me entering the mine means bending severely at the waist, and moving through it once we are inside often means getting down on all fours.

"The miners believe it is bad luck to have a woman in the mine," Juan Carlos says. "If a woman even gets too close to the entrance a lot of the miners will change mines, move on."

He sees the look I give Christine and adds, "Of course, you don't count, because they know you are laughing at our religion." He says this frankly, without judgment or blame.

We come, after a few hundred yards of crawling, to the "chapel," a small room dug into the rock where the miners worship Jesus Christ. We sit on rocks while Juan Carlos shows us how to chew the coca leaves. They taste like mud and produce way too much saliva, and it's all I can do not to gag.

"In the mine," Juan Carlos says, "we pray to Jesus Christ that he will protect us, we pray to the devil that he will bring us riches, and we pray to Baccha Mamma"—Mother Earth—"for everything, including our life."

We leave the little chapel and crawl on, the mine so narrow now I can't look up without banging my head, even on all fours, and when I do hunks of rock and dirt fall down behind me.

"What would happen right now," Christine says behind me, "if this were a movie, and we were Indiana Jones?"

"We must go up," says Juan Carlos, "to see the devil—Tio, we call him—and pay our respects."

A rickety ladder climbs the wall in front of us and disappears into an even darker room above.

Juan Carlos takes a deep breath through his nose. "Smell the gases?" he says. "Arsenic, selenium." My lantern is too close to Christine's handful of paper flags and they burst suddenly into flame, lighting the black walls around us.

Tio's chamber is bigger than Jesus's, and Tio himself much more colorful. He's made of some kind of plaster, painted brown with sparkling red eyes and long multicolored fingernails, a half-burned homemade cigarette stuck between fingers stained by nicotine. The platform he sits on is covered with offerings: bottles of alcohol, coca leaves, packs of cigarettes, dolls; the floor and walls of the room are drenched in what I suspect is llama blood.

Juan Carlos pulls a Marlboro out of his pocket, puts it in Tío's mouth, and lights it.

"The devil prefers Marlboros to the local cigarettes," he says. "They burn for such a long time."

After Tío's chamber the mine gets even narrower, and worse, it seems to be hollow as well. I hear a strange emptiness below me each time my knee hits the floor. We stop for breath in a slightly wider space and I ask Juan Carlos what is underneath us.

"Emptiness," he says, still smiling. "In the sixteen hundreds there were five thousand galleries operating in this mine. Now there are three hundred. There is no map. We just keep digging." He kicks a hole in the floor with his boot, drops a rock down it; we listen a long time before it thuds. "If there were ever an earthquake in Potosí," he says, slamming his hands together, "the whole mountain, boom, like a pancake."

We look at the rough-hewn walls around us, the caved-in timbers, the hole Juan Carlos's boot has made in the floor. "I think we get the feel of it," Christine says. "Thanks."

On our way out we pass miners entering and leaving, sometimes hauling hundred-pound sacks of rock on their backs. For each miner we pass, the drill is the same. We offer him alcohol. He spills some onto the ground for Baccha Mama. He drinks. We spill. We drink. We offer him coca leaves. He spills some, takes some, we do the same. He puts the cigarettes we give him into his hat. He says *Good day* and moves on.

When I can see daylight in front of me, I ask Juan Carlos if there was a temple we didn't see where the miners worship Baccha Mama.

Juan Carlos just laughs. "Baccha Mama is everywhere. We worship her every minute we are alive."

Back outside we take huge gulps of fresh air and try to rub the caked dirt off each other's faces. The miners want us to drink with them, so we do.

"You know, if this were America, this stuff we're drinking would have a skull and crossbones on it," Christine says, taking a big drink and passing the bottle to me.

The next day we fly east to the tropical lowlands and the burgeoning city of Santa Cruz. It is the "other place" in Bolivia, where the weather is warm, the women are beautiful, and life is a carnival all the time. We stay at the Hotel Los Tajebos, for all the world reminiscent of Acapulco in the late seventies: tropical birds and a bad mariachi band poolside and brunch on Sunday morning. We eat imported M&M's out of the minibar, and enjoy the air conditioning while it lasts.

Our guide in Santa Cruz is a no-nonsense woman named Mercedes. She gives us the city tour, tells us we say *gracias* like the Bolivian president, Jamie Paz Zamora, who was reared and educated in the United States. "Some people call him *Fifty Cents*," she says. "Some people say he tells lies."

Mercedes takes us to the zoo and shows us a statue of Noel Kempf Mercado, the zoo's founder, who was gunned down in the jungle when, looking for rare butterflies, he accidentally stumbled onto an illegal cocaine factory. "See this?" she says, pointing to a colorful snake coiled just on the other side of some chicken wire from Christine's feet. "They call that snake *ten minutes*. Know what I mean?"

Even the food is different in Santa Cruz, and at lunchtime the three of us plunge happily into a meal of the river fish they call *surubi*, uncooked but cured with lemon, ceviche-style. After lunch we go to El Fuerte, a pre-Inca archaeological site in the nearby Cordillera Oriental Range that is thought to have been a temple of matrimony in 1500 B.C. Mercedes shows us the ancient outlines of pumas and snakes, the twenty-four-seat altars where group marriages were performed.

"The triangular seats were for the women," Mercedes says, "the square seats for the men. We know this because the seat in the middle, where the high priest would have sat, is a square."

"What if the high priests were women?" Christine asks.

"Then those days were better than now." Mercedes says.

We stand at the foot of the ruin examining two parallel grooves in the granite that run the entire length of the structure and appear to shoot up into the sky.

"Erich von Daniken came here and proclaimed this a launching pad for spaceships," Mercedes says, cocking an eyebrow. "Visitation is up one hundred and fifty percent." I don't dare admit to her that I can see where he got the idea.

We fly back to La Paz for what we expect will be two quiet days of museums and churches, one last chance for Illimani to come out of the clouds. But when we arrive, Marcelo informs us he has pulled a few strings and we are going to his home-town of Oruro, three hours southeast of La Paz, because the best Carnival celebration in Bolivia has just begun there, and to waste the opportunity would be to tempt the gods. We have long ago stopped arguing with Marcelo, so we shower and climb into Ramone's Land Cruiser one last time.

Marcelo has told us how crowded Carnival will be; he has told us about the masks and costumes, which are so intricate and elaborate a dancer may spend a whole year's salary just to participate in the parade. He has told us about the dancing, the thousands of men and women of all ages who leap and swirl in unison, sometimes hundreds of them in one wavelike motion, for a minimum of ten hours along a parade route that covers eight miles.

What he has not told us about is the water balloons that children sell to the spectators by the thousands, nor the second most popular weapon, spray cans of sticky white foam. It doesn't take us long to figure out that the only defense is a strong offense, and soon, arms full of balloons and spray cans, every man, woman, and child in my line of vision is soaked to the skin. There is a purity in the Bolivians' fun at Carnival that is unmatched in my experience. I turn around just in time to see a man who must be eighty dump a bucket full of soapy water on Christine.

It is our last night in Bolivia. We are on our way back across the Altiplano from Carnival, wet, sticky, satiated with music and Paceña and dance. Marcelo and Ramone sing a song in Quechua that they know by heart. Marcelo has told me what the words mean: "The air is free, the water is free, why does the *creolo* think he can own the land?" Night is falling slowly, and out the car window on my side I can make out Orion's belt, upside down and in entirely the wrong position. The lights of suburban La Paz are on the horizon, but the bowl of lights that is the city will remain hidden until we reach the very edge.

Marcelo takes the pen from my hand and writes a long Quechua word in my diary:

Arusquipasopxanana-kasakipunirakisspawa.

He says, "In Quechua, all things can be communicated with this one word."

Christine gasps, and at first I think it's at the three-quarter moon that has just risen on the eastern horizon, but when I follow her gaze I see the four peaks of Illimani, tortured, magnificent, all 21,189 meters of her, finally cloudless in the fading light.

Eight Days in the Brooks Range with April and the Boys

It is 7:00 a.m. on Easter Sunday when we take off in a nine-seater airplane on a charter flight out of Fairbanks, Alaska, and our pilot, Fred, turns the nose to the north. North to the Brooks Range, north to the valley of the Sagavanirktok River, north to an airstrip two hundred miles above the Arctic Circle, a place still waist-deep in winter, the place we will sleep and eat and explore by dogsled for the next eight days.

It is a sparkling blue morning, and we fly low, first over the mighty Yukon River, then the smaller Koyakuk, then up into and among the peaks of the Brooks Range, in view of the Gates of the Arctic, and over the Chandalar Shelf. Still to the north is Atigun Pass, our corridor to the *other* side of the Brooks Range, and the frozen treeless netherworld of Alaska's North Slope.

I am traveling with my friends Roy and Janet, the two people most responsible for pulling me through a San Francisco winter fraught with too much loneliness and too much rain. Wild places have always healed me. But the prescription I've written again and again—high adventure combined with the dramatics of landscape—has an acid test in store for itself this time. It is Easter Sunday and I want a resurrection. I want to rise out of the mire of the most difficult winter of my life and sail over the arctic tundra on wings like a clear-headed angel.

"Nice place to be on Easter Sunday," Fred says, just at the moment it seems to me that our wingtips will brush the snow from the rock walls on either side of Atigun Pass, and I agree. I see the shadow our plane makes against a massive cornice, smaller than a speck of dust.

"Not much of a pass, really, is it?" he says, as the landscape opens below us and the snowy plain slopes northward toward the frozen Arctic Ocean. We can see a flat patch of snow that passes for an airstrip, and beside it two miniature pickup trucks, their engines making tiny exhaust clouds in the minus-eleven morning, one of them piled high with the boxes that make up a husky hotel.

"It makes you think people aren't meant to be up here," Fred says, "when the land makes them look that small."

As we step from the plane the blast of arctic air freezes the insides of our noses and eyes. We meet Brandon, our outfitter, who is wolfish and handsome. He's telling wilderness stories before the hellos are finished, full of a kind of energy that says, *This man was born to spend his life outdoors.*

Bill Mackey, the dog handler, offers only a shy hello. He is himself more sled dog than man, and bears the countenance of someone from another place, another century. He is quiet and kind with eyes that don't miss anything, that reveal an innate goodness, a knowledge of what it means to live well. His brother, Dave, and his father, Dick, are both Iditarod champions, and Bill places high in the years he chooses to run. He tends to each of the thirty-six dogs that will carry us as if this *were* the Iditarod. Seventy-two eyes stay fixed on him constantly as if at any moment he will start distributing T-bones. The dogs wag their tails in unison when he so much as looks in their direction, and they stand as tall as they can when he walks past them, hoping his hand might drop to their shoulder for a pat along the way.

While Brandon and Bill get the sleds ready, the rest of us fumble through our packs with rapidly freezing fingers and in moments we are more correctly layered than we have ever been our lives. On top I wear a Capilene undershirt, a long-sleeved pile T-shirt, a pile pullover, then another, a down vest, a Gore-Tex anorak, and finally a parka with a huge fur-rimmed hood. On the bottom it's Capilene, pile, pile, pile, and Gore-Tex. On my hands are silk liners, wool gloves, then down-and-leather mittens. On my head a neck gaiter, a balaclava, a face mask, and a bomber hat with flaps that close under my chin. My pack is almost empty, and the volume of the outfit I'm wearing is exceeded only by its value. I am leaning on a pickup truck two hundred miles above the Arctic Circle, and I've never been more expensively dressed in my life.

Brandon asks us if we've come with full water bottles, and when we say no, the look on his face gives us all a little lesson in respect for the place we find ourselves in. We have tried to outsmart the cold by bringing pencils instead of pens, and plenty of extra camera batteries. But something as simple as unfrozen water has never entered our minds.

"It's okay," Brandon says. "We'll make water first thing tonight in camp, after we get the tents set up and the stove going."

Bill's got the dogs divided into teams now and harnessed, and they are pulling hard at the sleds that are tied to the truck's bumpers with quick-release straps and anchored to the snow with big metal hooks. In a few moments we will leave the trucks behind and commit ourselves to eight days in a place where it's a big project to make a drink of water. The cold is already creeping into my fingers and toes.

Bill is showing me how my brake works, and where to put my feet and hands on the sled.

"April, Blue, Paint, Blackie, Silo," he says, pointing to one dog at a time. "If you lose their attention it's a good thing to call them by their names."

"Lose their attention?" I say.

"April is in your lead position. She's got a lot of village blood in her, a lot of Eskimo dog. It makes her very smart and a little hardheaded. If we pass caribou she may decide to kind of peel off." He makes an arc with his hand. "You might have to remind her . . ."

These are more words than Bill has spoken all day.

"Ready?" he says, and before I've nodded he's pulled the quick release and we're sailing along as if suddenly weightless. The sled, loaded to the gills with sleeping bags, camp gear, and dog food, skitters across the snow as if it's filled with feathers. I learn fast how to shift my weight like a water skier, how to lean into the corners and brace for the bumps, how to use the brake to keep from running over Blackie and Silo on the long downhills.

The dogs are running hard, pulling at their harnesses, tails wagging in time to each step. Every now and then April throws a glance over her shoulder at me, checking me out, and I try to maneuver the sled in a way that meets with her approval. When I have enough confidence to look behind me I see Janet and her dogs racing toward me, the same icy and surprised smile on her face that I know is on mine.

Surrounding us now there are only varying degrees of whiteness: the blue-white sky, the pure white tundra, the distant snow-deep mountain peaks, somehow whiter still. When I was a child flying in airplanes, I wanted nothing more than to climb out the window and jump into all that fluffy whiteness. The only thing that would have made it better, had I the power to imagine it, would have been to be pulled through that wonderland by a pack of smart and happy dogs.

"Stand on your brake hard!" comes Bill's voice from the front of the line, and I'm snapped back to the present just in time to see his sled disappear over the lip of a canyon. In seconds we *are* flying, straight down the side of a hill as long and as steep as anything I'd care to ski. It's all I can do to keep my sled behind the dogs, to stay upright myself at that speed, as the sled twists and leaps over bumps and drifts. Then the ground levels out and I dare to look up and I see we've entered a massive canyon decorated with the looping ribbon of a frozen river, punctuated with side canyons, narrow and dramatic, crowned to the south by a ring of deeply serrated peaks.

We stop at the bottom of the hill, breathless, amazed at ourselves for not falling, amazed even more by what's around us: infinity softened by sun. A cold wind blows upstream from the Arctic Ocean and cuts like a switchblade through all our layers.

"We'll make camp as soon as we hit the river," Bill says.

And the dogs leap to attention at the sound of his voice.

Our tents are called arctic ovens. They are big and well insulated, and they come equipped with tiny stoves. Since there are no trees on the North Slope we have brought enough Duraflame logs to burn one per evening. We follow Brandon's instructions to saw our log into three pieces, to burn one third at 9:30 p.m., one third at midnight, and the final third at 6:00 a.m. Though they smell a little toxic the logs are like miracles. We can sit in the tent in only two layers instead of five.

The next morning we leave our camp at the river and take the empty sleds across the Sagavanirktok Plain towards Atigun Gorge. The lightened sleds skid across the snow more easily than ever, and I am at my dogs' mercy, my brake having almost no effect. As mushers, we are improving, and Bill gets less careful about the terrain he chooses. By the time we've been underway for an hour we're bouncing over buried tundra tussocks and climbing and descending riverbanks and we've all face-planted at least one time.

We learn fast the single most important rule of dogsledding: Don't ever let go of the sled. The challenge is to remember this as we are falling, to make a dive for the runner with some part of our overclothed bodies, to let ourselves be dragged, the snow filling our parkas, our cameras bumping along underneath us, till we can get a leg back around to the runner, or claw with our arms up the back of our sleds.

Once we're inside Atigun Gorge the wind stills and the going gets easier. A small herd of caribou come down the hillside to greet us, curious. When they get our scent they spring straight into the air and bound away.

"If we're lucky we'll see Dall sheep in this canyon," Bill

says, and it's not five minutes until I do see them: eleven rams, no more than pinpoints on the horizon but unmistakable. It is better than winning the Publishers Clearing House Sweepstakes, being the one to spot those sheep, and I keep my eyes on the hillsides the whole rest of the day.

We see twenty-five sheep in all, and a set of wolverine tracks, and a whole flock of ptarmigan taking flight at once, still in their winter whites, only a touch of brown at the tips of their tails. We climb high enough to get a glimpse of the pipeline, snaking its surreal way across the horizon on its path to the oil fields in Prudhoe Bay.

We are almost back down to the mouth of the canyon when something makes me look up, and I see what Brandon calls "the big guy in the brown suit" on the horizon. A full-grown grizz, all eight feet and 750 pounds of him, keeping up with us at an easy lope just one layer of canyon formation above. Adrenaline surges through me and I shout to Bill, wave my arms to Janet, lose my sled and drop my camera, wind up stuck waist-deep in snow and stranded, but still getting to watch him run across the top of the scree. The blond tips of his dark coat gleam in the sunlight, and the rhythm of his lope makes a mantra in my head: *life is good, life is good*. We watch him climb to the next-higher layer of canyon, then up and over a frozen waterfall and beyond the canyon rim.

Already, I am thinking of these dogs as mine. April is my brilliant child, bossy, confounding, a little aloof. Blue is the melancholy one, the poet, with eyes the color of glacier water in June. Silo is my bruiser, always picking fights with Blackie, who is the invisible one, wholly dedicated to the task of turning dog power into mileage mushed. And Paint . . . Paint is my special child, a product of accidental inbreeding. He's sweet and lovable and dumb as a box of rocks. Mornings, when we are about to take off, he barks so hard he flips himself over, tangling his harness so badly that we are always the last sled to leave.

On the third day, it's warmer, and the river ice has an inch or more of water on top that sloshes between the feet of the dogs. The ice groans and creaks under the weight of the sled and April slows a little, feeling her way across ground she's not sure is solid. Paint misunderstands and keeps barreling into her, behavior she corrects with a couple of nips to his ears.

Up until now the rivers have been frozen white and crystalline, but today for the first time we see a hint of blue below the surface. At one place the water has pushed the ice up, welled itself into an igloo shape, fifteen feet high and gleaming, and I wonder about our nearness to it, and watch it for a sign.

"Spring's a-comin'," is all Bill says when we go by.

When we turn back for camp below a peak they call Cloud, we make a figure eight with the sleds that is truly a thing of beauty: the bright colors of our Gore-Tex, the crisscrossing of the sleds, the thin line of dogs reaching homeward against all that vast bright white.

Then April finds a caribou carcass and dives for it, the rest of the team close in tow. They get so tangled I have to unhook Blue before I can move them, and Blue, an escape artist, wriggles free of my hands. I dive for him successfully, but wind up facedown in the caribou carcass. Paint thinks this is a wonderful game and dives hard on top of me, Silo close on his heels. We are all so tangled, my dogs and I, that Brandon has to rescue us. I can hear Roy's happy laughter behind me. From the top of a nearby hill, Bill waits and watches, graceful, even when his sled is still. In the cock of his head there is more than amusement; even at this distance he sees everything essential his dogs are giving to me. In minutes we're back up and traveling. April grins at me over her shoulder. I want this trip never to end.

In the evenings we sit in the cook tent and tell stories. Brandon's got beautiful forearms and crazy eyes and tells a better story than anyone I have ever known, though both Roy and I take turns trying to give him a run for his money. I've got the range, and Roy's got the ruthlessness, but Brandon's got a cast of Alaskan bushmen, better sound effects than Universal Studios, and a penchant for turning a day hike into a life-threatening event. The only thing that interrupts the stories is the barking during Bill's nightly feeding, and we wait to take up the talking until we've heard the after-dinner chorus, thirty-six little voices, howling their thanks.

On Day Four we break camp and travel farther up-valley, through a place where the whole Sagavanirktok River squeezes through a slot canyon, above which lies a whole new landscape of steeper canyon walls and higher peaks. We spend hours moving on ice which is today wetter still and covered with thin sheets of crust that shatter under the dogs' feet into shapes like petals, the sleds leaving the softest trail imaginable in their wake.

I am grateful for the way this landscape demands my whole attention, how it forces me at every moment out of my head and into it, how once I'm in it, it's impossible for me to feel alone.

The day gets warmer and warmer until we shed our parkas

completely and change our hats for headbands. The ground starts to smell like springtime and the ice gets bluer still. By the time we get to camp I am down to only three layers, and after we set the tent up we lie on the ice in front of it and take in the most spectacular 360-degree view of our adventure-filled lives. We could be at Club Med, the sun on our faces is so warm.

We spend the next two days exploring the high valleys of the Sagavanirktok, watching herd after herd of caribou move north for the summer, watching the snow melt, watching the river turn blue as Blue's eyes.

"If we don't get out now we're here for the summer," Bill says the next morning, and he turns out to be right. On our trip back down the valley, water stands eight inches deep on top of ice so thin it crackles. April slows, almost to a stop sometimes, and the muscles in my legs tense for the fall. Where there were fifty ice heaves on the way upriver, there are now five hundred, and the snow on the south face of even the highest peaks is all but gone. When we get to the slot canyon, water is thundering down the surface of the ice and around the boulders, and I maneuver the sled between them like a raft on a river, April and the boys in belly-deep and swimming for home.

When we get back to our first base camp the river is broken free and running strong behind the tent site. This will be the first night we don't need to melt snow for drinking water; it will be the first night we eat dinner outside. When I take April's harness off she lets me rub her belly until the sun has dried it, and she falls sound asleep under my hand. I look up to find Bill watching, that same *good dog* look in his eye.

Brandon has saved his coup d'état story for this, our last night together: the time his wife shot him through the neck with a .22 on their honeymoon. We watch the late-spring sun roll not towards the horizon but along it; for several nights now it hasn't gotten truly dark. The dropping temperature sends us toward bed, but then the northern lights come out and we run in place to keep warm while we watch them, their liquid green translucence made even more ghostly by the twilight as they dance across the sky.

When the light show is over, Bill takes me aside. "If you ever decide you want your own dog team," he says, "you come see me about it," and I nod and shake his hand.

It is a brief exchange, one good dog to another, but possibility washes through me like good medicine, and I go to sleep dreaming of six little Aprils of my own.

The next morning there is nothing to do but pack up the tents and begin the long mush up and out of the canyon. We climb the canyon wall slowly, our sleds suddenly cumbersome and heavy, and we run along behind the dogs to help them with the load. What had been an all-white landscape on Easter Sunday is suddenly fraught with color, the brown tundra, the black mountaintops, the snake of river now almost sapphire in the sun. But when we reach the canyon rim we find plenty of snow still standing, and the minute the ground levels the dogs begin again to fly.

In this moment I feel only two things: the cold wind in my face and my own deep happiness. I am moving from light into light on a surface purer than air and kinder than water. I am thankful for the holy shimmer of these backlit peaks and top-heavy cornices and for the way the wind howls around them.

For the crack of the ice under padded dog paws and the water that bubbles below. For the feathered emerald ghost dance of the northern lights in the forever twilight of an Alaskan evening. For the way April offers first one leg, then the other, to the morning's harness and my hand.

In Bhutan
There Is No Way
to Be Famous

There is a mountain the Bhutanese people call Jhomol-hari, 24,500 feet high and marking the border between the tiny Himalayan kingdom of Bhutan and Tibet. The mountain is named for the mountain goddess, Jhomo, and is sacred, like all mountains in Bhutan, but even a little more so. No one is allowed to climb the mountain, but there is a nine-day trek that runs from the town of Paro, Bhutan, three days up to a base camp thirteen thousand feet high at the foot of the mountain goddess and then over a sixteen-thousand-foot pass to a remote monastery called Lingshi. Then it's up and over another sixteen-thousand-foot pass back to the capital of Bhutan, Thimpu, and the windy river road to Paro, where the trek begins.

The guidebook says that trekking in the kingdom of Bhutan is different from trekking in other parts of the Himalayas. It says: *Here there is no easygoing trekking.* It says the climate is much windier, colder, and damper than in Nepal, and that the treks start at least three thousand feet higher. It says there are no indoor facilities of any kind and none of the routes are marked, that the trails cross narrow valleys and steep gorges and are on the flats so infrequently that in a day when the net elevation gain is two or three thousand feet you will have actually climbed and descended seven thousand feet or more. It says emergency medical evacuation is logistically impossible and that leeches are a consideration.

Then it says this: *But if you want to walk through wild unspoiled country on routes where you will likely not meet another westerner the entire way* . . . It says: *If you are a true adventurer* . . .

I am trying, these days, to be something other than a true adventurer, to be more like a grown-up, to give up my dreams of places like Antarctica and Mongolia, or if not to give them up entirely, then to choose adventures that are safer, more predictable, less close to the razor's edge. It has something to do with the mid-thirties, perhaps. Something to do with the people I have met abroad who seem vacant and hollow—little more than the lists of their adventures, which they will happily chronicle for even the most casual acquaintance. Something to do with being afraid that like them, all I'll have to show at the end of my life is a drawer full of canceled passports with really impressive stamps. Something to do with beginning to value my life.

I have broken so many bones, been want-to-die sick in faraway places so often, have thought *Well, there are worse ways to go* so many times as the backcountry snow begins to slide or the wave engulfs my boat, that those life-threatening moments have almost lost their power to move me.

Here you go again, the voice says inside me, as I dangle from a rope on a thousand-foot cliff or swim for my life next to an overturned boat in the middle of a class 5 rapid, and even in that moment of panic the voice is a little bored. *Now you are in love*, it says, *now you have a mortgage. You have horses and dogs that depend on you to feed them, and friends—real friends—these days who would care a lot if you didn't come home.* The voice is bored with the hardest thing, the most difficult way, in the most dangerous season. The voice wants to slow down the pace of my adventures. *Haven't you always liked walking?* it says, which is how I started thinking about Bhutan.

There was a time in my life when I thought walking wouldn't have counted as an adventure, when the word *adventure* had to mean strapping myself into expensive apparatus (downhill skis, a kayak, roller blades) and going extremely fast. Faster, in fact, than everybody else. If it wasn't dangerous, and it wasn't competitive, as far as I was concerned it wasn't a sport. These were not things I said out loud, but I believed them, and I raged against myself if I shrank, even inwardly, from the danger, or if I failed to finish some self-invented competition in first place.

I'm trying to give all that up, my addiction to danger and my absurdly competitive edge, but it still exists inside me. And all the other parts of travel—my thrill at seeing new places, my deep craving for the unknown and unexpected that is a part of every trip, my excitement over the curves of unpronounceable letters on the nose of a foreign airplane, or even the smell of fresh ink in my passport—are things I'm not sure I *want* to give up.

For all of these reasons, Bhutan seems like the perfect destination. As unknown a place as there is on earth. A country with an outfitted-trips-only policy (if you aren't on an organized trek they won't let you out of the airport) that will reduce the life-threatening factor significantly—there is only so much trouble the guide will let me get myself into. A walking trip that will allow me to prove to myself that walking is a sport, was perhaps *the* original sport before we all got seduced by the thrill of speed and the win.

One foot in front of the other, up to the top of the mountain pass and down. There is something pure about it, unencumbered by gear or rules or devices, unaided by lifts or wheels or even currents; only the simple law of gravity working for or against me, only my mind and my body to speed me up or slow me down. I've always said four miles an hour is exactly the right pace to see a landscape, and now I'll have a chance to prove my words true.

I convince myself that the measure of how good my relationship is is that it will weather Bhutan beautifully, that my dogs will be fine and that one of the things my friends love about me is that I send them postcards from places they have to get out the atlas to find. I convince myself that I can take this adventure safely, that I can get every immunization, carry the world's largest first-aid kit, put the odds in my favor all the way. I console all the old needs with the incessant up and down and the leeches that the guidebook promised. I am compensating for the low degree of difficulty of a walking trip, I tell myself, with the extreme remoteness of the place.

Above all else I keep thinking about the sunrise on the Himalayas, about walking in a whole mountain range of peaks more than 23,000 feet high, about being the only westerner at a Buddhist festival at a mountain monastery older than anything I've ever known. I think about how magical the word *Bhutan* sounds in my mouth.

Bhutan's entire air fleet consists of two British Aerospace 146 jets that seat seventy-two people each. There's a jolly pilot from New York called Captain George and a handful of Bhutanese pilots he's training so that in a few years he will be, in his own words, obsolete. Druk Air (a *druk*, in Bhutanese, is a dragon and the national symbol) flies from Bangkok to Paro, Bhutan, on Wednesdays, Fridays, and Sundays, and from Paro to Bangkok on the other days, unless one of the planes is down or the weather is bad, and then it's anybody's guess when you'll get in or out.

It's a cloudy day when I arrive, no views of the Himalayas, but when we break through the lowest cloud layer I notice we are flying between the walls of a tortured and steep-walled canyon. Captain George gets on the loudspeaker and says, "Good afternoon, ladies and gentlemen. In a few minutes it will appear to you that I am going to shave off the tops of several trees on the south side of the canyon, but we do it just this way every day, so please don't be alarmed." I think, *Why would anybody ever build an airport in the bottom of a canyon*, and then it dawns on me that I may be looking at the biggest flat spot in Bhutan, and I *feel* like I'm in the Himalayas even if I haven't seen them yet.

My guide meets me at the airport. His name is Karma. He has soft hands, a shy smile, and such a willingness to be present in every conversation that we will become fast friends in the month we are together. Karma, like all Bhutanese men, wears a *gho*, the mandatory national dress, with knee socks and what I would call black Buster Browns that make him look, from the back, like a member of a women's varsity field hockey team.

In the next thirty days Karma and I will talk about everything in the world, from arranged marriages to Bill Clinton, from racial tension to sex with the lights on, from the origins of Buddhism to how, if you live in a country with an ocean, you manage to hide your erections on the beach. A few months earlier Karma found himself on the short end of an arranged marriage, his girlfriend of five years forced to marry another man who will make, in his life, more money than Karma. "She was not entirely displeased," Karma will say, in a voice less bitter than sad.

Karma and I go straight from the airport to the Paro Dzong, which is a fortress and a monastery, huge and white and adorned with intricate woodcarvings and painted buttresses. Karma gets special permission from a monk for us to enter one of the prayer rooms, and we take our shoes off and go in. Every bit of wall space is covered with murals in soft blues and pinks and yellows. Strips of silk of every primary color hang from the ceilings, and the floors are hard warm wood with cracks in them that are four centuries old. It would take more than a day just to notice all the detail of the artwork in this room.

The late-afternoon sun pours in through the windows and lights the altar where every morning the caretaker brings in a bowl of water for the Buddha, and every night before prayer he throws it away. Karma whispers to me the story of how Buddhism came to Bhutan, and I can imagine a hundred red-robed monks saying their evening prayers here and I think, *If these had been my prayer rooms, I'd be religious too.*

Tshe dato, tshe chima. What you do now is what you get later—what we call karma—is the philosophy the Bhutanese live by. They live, therefore, with honesty and kindness, in a constant state of gratitude for what they have. Karma explains, without a hint of judgment, that this is why the Bhutanese don't need therapists and lawyers. "We take our time here," he says. "It takes time to appreciate what we have." No one is in a hurry, anywhere we go, and what's even more astonishing is that although I see hundreds of babies, I never hear one cry.

"There is no way to be famous in Bhutan," Karma says. "I think that makes it easier on everyone."

Karma teaches me how to say hello in Bhutanese—*Koo zoo zam po-la* (you add the *la* if you wish to show respect)—and thank you: *Ga den che.* Everything he says begins to sound profound to me and I stay up late trying to remember and write down his words. I scribble, "Soup is compulsory," one night in my journal, only partly believing that he is talking about his outfitter's menu.

In Thimpu, Bhutan's largest city and home to thirteen thousand people, there are two human stoplights, the only stoplights of any kind in Bhutan. In the middle of a four-way intersection, in formal military dress, a young man stands inside a kiosk, white gloves on his hands and silver whistle around his neck, directing with a flourish the sporadic traffic that comes from all four sides. He is more machine than man in his movements, more performance artist than civil servant. "We had electric stoplights for a while," Karma says, "but we found that sometimes people had to stop needlessly, and so we had them removed."

There are prayer flags everywhere we go, thousands of them, decorating the towns and houses, the mountain passes and the fields, attached to their handmade flagpoles and reaching upwards, ten, twenty, sometimes a hundred feet to the sky. White for air, yellow for ether, red for fire, green for earth, blue for water: always in that order for safe passage and good luck. I go into a store in Thimpu and buy my own set of prayer flags to hang on Yele La—the higher of the two passes on the trek—if I make it to the top.

I spend the first two weeks of my stay in Bhutan visiting monasteries with Karma, acclimating to the altitude and food and water, trying to slow myself down to Bhutanese time and still push myself hard enough to stay in shape for Jhomolhari.

Some of the monasteries dangle impossibly from cliffs; one sits right on top of a tumbling river. We time our visits with the annual festivals in Thimpu and Jakar and get to watch hours of dancing, men in multicolored robes and the heads of demons and deer, women in traditional dresses called *kiras*, all of them repeating and repeating steps for hours, acting out dramas that are nearly as old as time.

I am struck by how much these people touch each other; children, teenage boys, old women, all of them drape their arms around each other when standing or walking, and I can see on their faces that they believe in their ability to hold each other up.

We stay the nights, on the journey, in Bhutanese guest-houses, which like most houses in Bhutan are big and colorful and beautifully decorated. My room in one house has two beds, a table, and a perfectly carved and painted bench. The walls, starting from the floor up, are painted in bands of orange, light green, darker green, patterned orange and yellow, dark blue, light blue, light yellow, then red, green, orange, yellow, and blue again, and the blunt ends of the roof beams are painted with dragons and flowers and bolts of lightning.

I think of how many weeks it must have taken to paint this one room, how many days to carve a pole for one prayer flag, how many years to paint just one of the intricate murals that cover the insides of the monasteries, and wonder if this isn't another reason there aren't any lawyers or therapists in Bhutan.

There is no electricity in the houses, none in most of the valleys, which are deep and beautiful and ringed by pine forests. There is no indoor plumbing, only candlelight and quiet. At sunset we sit on handwoven blankets laid over hard wooden benches, drinking tea and rice wine and watching darkness fall outside the window.

There are a few rules of personal behavior in this country, and though Karma is almost too polite to tell me when I'm doing something wrong, I've learned that whenever he begins a sentence with *actually*, I'm screwing up somehow. I learn to walk around all sacred objects clockwise. I learn never to point with my finger, only to indicate with my whole hand. Since my feet are the least sacred part of my body I must never show anyone their soles, so when I sit on the floor, as we often do, I must tuck my legs underneath me. I may never enter a temple with my sleeves rolled up, and because I am a woman I have to wear ankle-length skirts all the time, even when I'm trekking. When I give or receive a gift I must always do so with both hands.

In the town of Tongsa we are invited to one of the high rituals inside the monastery's innermost temple, complete with six-foot-long horns and drums called *ngas*, and sea shells to blow through and a million candles burning on every available space. The old monks chant while the young ones in the back rows fall easily into trance and the even younger ones in the front rows stare at me, all giggles and big eyes.

In the Buddhist temple at Kurjey, where only kings and queens can visit, I am so overwhelmed by the beauty of the giant statues that I ask Karma to teach me how to pray, and he does. Everything in threes: hands above the head, then at the mouth, then at the heart, then hands on the ground, knees on the ground, head on the ground and up, a minimum of three times; there is no maximum.

In the third-oldest temple in Bhutan I let the monks put on my back a piece of chain mail made in the thirteenth century by a monk named Pema Lingpa, and I make three circles around the temple carrying it, though it must weigh a hundred pounds. If I do this, they tell me, I will get my wish.

Later Karma asks me what my wish is and I tell him: to make it through the trek alive and well, to learn all the lessons Bhutan has to teach me, to get home safe to my dogs, my friends, and my sweetheart, to find them all safe on the other side of the world.

On our journey from festival to festival I hear so many stories of Buddha and other enlightened figures in the history of the religion that they all start to blend together. One Zen master turned himself into a tiger, another read every book ever written, another could win over the hearts of dogs with his songs.

The story that stands out most of all—the one that is meant to stand out most of all—is the story of Gautama, the first

Buddha, who was sequestered all his early life by his father the king. The king believed the best way to groom his son (who was the result of an immaculate conception when the queen had a dream about a white elephant) was to keep him completely cut off from the pain and suffering in the world. But the future Buddha sneaked out of the palace one night and roamed the streets of the kingdom, finding suffering, old age, sickness, and death everywhere. His newfound knowledge of pain made him want to know first why it existed, and then what he could do to prevent it, so he put the whole town to sleep one night and stole away from his father's house on a horse whose feet didn't touch the ground.

He lived as a poor man from then on, begging for what he needed to survive. After many years of sacrifice, learning, practice, and meditation, when the one who would become Buddha achieved enlightenment, he reached down and touched the ground in front of him, because he wanted the earth to bear witness to the moment. We see him represented most often this way, in the lotus position, one hand in his lap or around his begging bowl, the other reaching down to touch the earth.

This was the story I would remember most clearly, not only because it seemed to justify my need for travel, but also because whenever I have achieved what feels like the tiniest bit of enlightenment, it has always been in the presence of—if not in direct response to—some beautiful place on earth.

Jhomolhari Trek: Day One
Paro Druk
7,300 feet

It's 6:00 a.m. in the Paro Druk Hotel, site of the only double bed in Bhutan. (When Karma saw it he said, "You can sleep in this bed in any direction you wish.") My fellow trekkers arrived yesterday and are asleep in other rooms: Beth, the marathon runner from Manhattan and her brand-new husband, Doug; Frank and Carly, world travelers from upstate New York; and Sanjay Saxena, our Indian-American guide from San Francisco, who will share guiding responsibilities with Karma for the rest of the trip.

Beth's bag didn't arrive, which sent her into a tearful panic, and Frank said, in front of Karma, how glad he was that we had an American guide. Carly told us she married Frank on the condition that he would be away from home 120 days a year; and we thought she meant *no more than*, but it turned out to be *at least*. Overall, though, we seem like a pretty amicable group.

In spite of the double bed, I'm not sleeping. The weather has been terrible, rain down here, snow in the high country almost constantly, and Karma told us that last year's attempt at this trek got stranded for four days and then the trekkers were turned back by deep snow. I've walked in bad weather for nine days before, but never in a country that didn't own a helicopter, and never at even close to sixteen thousand feet. I've been two weeks in the Himalayas and still not a day clear enough to see the high peaks.

In the hallway outside my room a barefoot monk is walking, chanting, and waving a creaking ball of incense. He will go to every corner of the sleeping hotel and bless it, the way the night workers at an airport Sheraton might vacuum the rug.

Day One (later)
Shana
9,482 feet

Today's walk was easy, up the gradual Paro River Valley through villages of no more than two or three houses and farms where the men use oxen to plow the fields and the women beat wheat with handmade brooms. Brilliantly colored chilies were laid out to dry on every rooftop, brightest red and green against the steel-gray slate. The horsemen walked with us, and one old man whose function is unclear to me, and who looks like Charlie Chan, carried an umbrella. The horses were weighed down with folding card tables and propane tanks and ridiculous amounts of our gear.

We stopped to pick peas at one of the farms for dinner, and Frank bought a couple of pheasants from some older boys on the trail. Later, Karma and I passed through a village where five brothers and sisters, ages four to eight, were playing in a small religious shrine called a *stupa*. They were so beautiful, even by Bhutanese standards, and Karma coaxed them into singing for us. The sunset, the *stupa*, the children singing like sweet bells chiming, and all of it in the middle of a muddy cow pasture. It made me understand why I still hadn't heard a child cry in this country, why I'd rarely seen an adult frown.

The trails are, except for the yak shit, clean and trash-free, the outfitters all adhering scrupulously to a pack-it-in, pack-it-out, no-fire-ring policy, trying to learn from the ruination of the trails in their neighboring Nepal. King Jigme Singye Wangchuck (the Bhutanese call him simply His Majesty) is famous for saying, "I don't want to increase the gross national product, I want to increase the gross national happiness." He says money makes people crazy, no matter how much of it you have, and happiness is all that matters. He has shut down all the country's lumberyards and strip mines, and has instituted a daily tourist fee (two hundred dollars per person) that more than picks up the slack. He strictly limits the number of tourists per year, is actively keeping television out of Bhutan, and has instituted a kind of Bhutanese Arbor Day, when every citizen is supposed to plant a tree.

The cook on our trek, nicknamed Cocktu, is at least part magician, given what he has to work with. He serves up every dish of wild mushrooms or chicken and greens with a flourish, a radish or a cucumber cut into the shape of a half-moon or a rose. The staples are right up my alley, the *ama datsi*, which is chilies and cheese, the *kawwa datsi*, which is chilies and potatoes, and the *shamoo datsi*, which is chilies and mushrooms, are ever-present, all of it just on the border of too-hot-to-eat. The chilies are, I think, what has kept me winning the constant battle in my stomach between the good bugs and the bad bugs, but I fear I'm losing ground. Cocktu and his assistants are hacking with something that sounds very like bronchitis, so I imagine it won't be long before we get that too.

It's raining steadily and has been most of the day, and tonight, alone in my tent, I'm torn between my fear that I'll get too sick to make it to sixteen thousand feet twice in three days and a hope that I'll get so sick I'll have to give up graciously and turn back.

Beth's bag caught up to us via yak today, which made her very happy and impressed all of us. She and I are getting friendly and a little competitive, though as usual the competition factor may be entirely in my head. We are both in better shape than the other Americans, including Sanjay, which causes him some discomfort and a little anger. All the Bhutanese can walk twice as far as we can, and in less than half the time. Frank is in great shape for his age, but he doesn't listen to instructions and he seems to have taken a particular dislike to me. The best people in the world would be edgy in this weather. Karma warns us that tomorrow's walk is much harder than today's.

Day Two
Soi Thangthanka
11,745 feet
Okay.

Picture a jungle, then put it at eleven thousand feet, then make it rain for three weeks prior to your visit so that the trail is knee-deep in mud 80 percent of the time. Then picture rocks, big green slippery moss-covered rocks, spaced just too far apart to jump between, then picture it raining nonstop all day, pouring down as though the machine up in heaven is broken. Then picture wiping out, first thing in the morning, as you try to jump from one of those moss-covered rocks to the other, falling forward with your camera in one hand and your water bottle in the other. Picture the knot rising instantly, the size of a lemon on your shin where it made contact with granite, and then imagine the blood mixing with the rain and the mud and the yak shit, and imagine trying to clean it with your mud-soaked bandanna. Then imagine walking thirteen more miles, up the sides of cliffs, sometimes so steep that you are setting off little mud slides as you go, and then, just for fun, imagine doing all of that in an ankle-length skirt.

That was our day, under clouds that were much too low to let us see the mountains. I'm sure it dawned on each of us in our own little watery worlds that if the weather continues this way we could do this whole damn walk to sixteen thousand feet twice without seeing the mountain we've come to see.

The Buddhists would say this is our opportunity to practice nonattachment. For me it's just another opportunity to prove how I thrive in the face of adversity. I am absurdly good at this, and the more miserable the conditions, the more I seem to excel. I've been the first one to camp, two days running, just slightly ahead of Beth and Doug. At dinner Karma told me that the staff were all talking about my walking stamina, and that, as usual, has made me inordinately happy. Way happier, I know, than it should.

Frank, on the other hand, wound up in Tibet today, after Karma and Sanjay each told us at least a thousand times to stay to the right of all the *stupas* because the road to the left went to Tibet and we'd be arrested as soon as we hit the border and the trek would be over for everyone. We sat there on our lunch break, first waiting for Frank and then going ahead and eating, each of us knowing, none of us saying, that he had gone to Tibet. When he finally showed up, two hours later, having gotten almost to the border and then at the last second miraculously been turned back by some Bhutanese soldiers, he blamed Karma and Sanjay for not being clear.

I'm in my tent now, with my tea and my Walkman, the Crash Test Dummies asking, "Is this a parable or a very subtle joke?" A half an hour ago the rain stopped driving against the side of the tent and I opened the flap to send a joyful cry toward the other tents and got a mouthful of snowflakes.

Seven more days. Five days of trekking and two rest days. One hundred and sixty-eight hours till the trek is over, two hundred and forty hours until I'm in Bangkok and can get *phad thai* and a massage.

Here and now though, there is a boy named Doten, the cook's assistant, who brings us tea and a basin of water to wash with in the morning, and the smile on his face is full of such goodness it is impossible to believe that when the trek is over we will have to find a way to face the day without him.

Karma says I'm crazy for counting hours the way I do and living in the future. When you ask a Bhutanese person how long until something happens—the arrival at a destination, for instance—the answer will be, always, "We will be there after *some time*."

If it snows as hard as it's been raining it could mean we aren't going anywhere. Sanjay says tomorrow's walk is even harder, but I don't see how it can be. He also says when we get above the last farmhouse, the women don't have to wear skirts anymore.

Day Three
Jangothang
13,288 feet

Right at this minute I am staring at a 24,500-foot mountain goddess and it's a good thing I'm writing because if I had to speak I could not. It's not only her height that is so impressive, it's also her girth. She fills up the head of this valley as though God found this place to drop the biggest rock in creation, almost twelve thousand feet taller than the valley floor and twice that far across, his/her way of saying, *You've reached the end of the road.*

The sun is shining. I woke up at 5:00 a.m., unzipped my tent window, and there she was, the most magnificent mountain I've ever laid eyes on in a perfectly clear dawn. All day we've been walking up the valley toward her, moving in and out of her sight as the river twists and turns.

We stopped for lunch at a farmhouse and I could hardly eat mine fast enough, seeing the sun, knowing that another seven miles up-valley would land us at her feet. I walked up and up through wide yak pastures, bonsai pines wind-sculpted along the riverbank, thick carpets of tundra moss stretching from canyon wall to canyon wall. Then all of a sudden I rounded a corner and there she was, not her peak, like we'd seen in the morning, or glimpses of ridgelines that we got throughout the day, but all of her.

I can't believe what the low afternoon light is doing to this mountain. Right now there is a band of light across her middle, lit sideways by the setting sun, the peak snow-laden and splitting into a thousand crevasses against the deepest blue sky, and the glaciers, gray-white and blue, are tumbling down her sides out of the bottoms of the clouds.

There's a fort near the camp that was built when an ancient king called all the village people together and told them to remove the mountain because the sun was setting behind it much too early in the day. The people decided it would be easier to kill the king than remove the mountain, so they planned a revolution and he built himself the fortress, but they got him in the end anyway.

I reached camp first again and just because I was feeling so damn cocky I decided to run up to the bottom of the glacial moraine, another eight hundred vertical or so and a three-hour turnaround, which I'm sure put me above fourteen thousand feet. I got close enough to touch the base of the goddess, but I didn't dare, which Karma says was the right decision. I'm higher than I've ever been, and so far no sign yet of AMS (acute mountain sickness).

We're having a birthday party for Doug tonight—right now the cooks are baking a cake in a hole in the ground using a wood fire and two of our washbasins—and tomorrow is a rest day.

Day Four
Jangothang
13,288 feet

I'm doing something today that is very hard for me: I'm spending the rest day resting.

Sanjay got us up at 5:00 a.m. for the alpenglow on the mountain, then we placed bets on what time the sun would hit camp and I won with 7:25. Then we had a leisurely and wonderful breakfast, said goodbye to our horsemen and hello to the yak herders (yaks do far better than horses above thirteen thousand feet).

The herd of yaks broke loose from their tether around ten and tried to stampede us, and Beth and I found a comfortable rock to lie on and soak up the sun. We read to each other from the books we brought, mine the Zen-influenced poems of Jane Hirschfield, hers the ageless wisdom of the *Tao Te Ching*, and she broke out some chocolate-covered espresso beans that she had sneaked into Doug's pack. Then it was time for lunch and now it has somehow become four, and I'm rested and still reasonably healthy (though nearly everybody else is sick with something) and ready as I'll ever be to tackle the first pass as we turn away from Jhomolhari and really start to climb.

We're all a little nervous about tomorrow. The yaks are insane and I fear for my luggage, but I can't carry the things I really care about (my shot film and cassette tapes) without sacrificing the things (Gore-Tex and dry socks and fleece mittens) that might keep me alive if a storm should blow through. I'm fighting so hard to stay healthy, but it seems impossible with the cook sneezing into the food and the yak shit everywhere, and trying to keep my leg from becoming infected and Doug (who's got severe diarrhea) passing around his birthday champagne, and Frank, who doesn't believe in doing any of the things we are supposed to do to keep us from infecting ourselves and each other, and my period, just arrived to make my defenses low.

The mountain towers above us, impassive, mind-boggling, majestic, and tomorrow if it's clear we will see two more, though neither as big or important as she. The barometer on Frank's watch says *rain* (we hate Frank's watch) and it was cold last night—under twenty degrees—but it's warm enough right now for Beth to be shaving her legs in the washbasin and for us all to do a little laundry and stretch our wet clothes across the warm rocks to dry.

Day Five
Negla La (La *means pass*)
15,781 feet

LHA JAALO! LHA JAALO! That's what Karma says we're supposed to shout when we get to the top of a pass. LHA JAALO! Karma says it's probably a record: two and a half hours, ten miles, 2,500 feet vertical. It's cloudy again, gray all around us and not a peak in sight. Except for the multicolored prayer flags marking the pass, we could be on the surface of the moon.

Day Five (later)
Lingshi
12,992 feet

Right now, sitting in a folding chair at Lingshi, I could say there was really nothing to it. Yeah, I got a little dizzy. Yeah, every so often this thing would happen where my legs felt like lead. Yeah, Beth caught me right before the summit—those four New York City Marathons kicking in, no doubt—but for the last few weeks I've been so consumed with worry about whether or not I'd make it, and today my only worry was whether or not I'd make it first.

We're camped below the Lingshi Dzong, one of the world's most remote monastery. There are only a few people here, and yak herders and their families live in spooky black tents made of yak hair that get battered by the wind in these high pastures. We passed a tent today where a woman and two little girls stood at the door staring out at us, and each of us, I know, bundled and piled in our Gore-Tex, tried to imagine a whole life above tree line with nothing between us and the elements except a thick piece of hide.

Tonight at dinner Frank waited until all the cooks were sitting at the table and then said, "Who would have thought these people would know enough to cut a cucumber into the shape of a flower?"

Tomorrow was supposed to be a rest day, but there is a

group of Germans coming and Sanjay wants to stay ahead of them, so we go on instead, over the Yele La, which is only a hundred feet higher than the Negla La, but all the guides say it's a much harder pass. I have finally developed the Bhutanese cough, a low guttural thing that makes me feel, for a moment, like my chest is about to split in half, and all of us are making pretty quick trips to the latrine. I'm going to do that now, before it gets dark, and re-dress my leg and look for some cough drops. I think we are all secretly feeling that losing our rest day may be a mistake.

Day Six
A meadow just shy of the Yele La
15,700 feet

We are having lunch, one major push (about three hundred feet) short of the Yele La. On the way up here I got a sharp and deep pain in my chest, like I'd been kicked by the hoof of a very large animal. It stunned me, nearly knocked me down, so I sat and took deep breaths for about twenty minutes and drank a bottle of water while Beth held my hand and said comforting things until the pain went away . . . nearly.

Everything's okay now, but there's one major climb to go and I'm scared. All Sanjay had to say was "Heartburn?" which is unlikely since I haven't been able to keep any food in my system for more than ten minutes in two days. Then I remembered how much my arms were tingling yesterday, and how I thought nothing of it then and just loosened the straps on my pack. I thought I was prepared for everything, but my heart was something I never considered. There was no way I could have been prepared for this.

I looked out at the peaks a moment ago, the glaciers all around us, the unbelievable vastness of these high meadows, and said, for the thousandth time in my life, "Well, I guess this wouldn't be a bad place to go"; but it was someone else's voice saying it, not mine anymore. I want to go home to my love and my friends; I want to live on to see Antarctica and Mongolia. I think about the pleasure I got on the days I cruised into camp just ahead of Beth and I want to slap myself silly. Was it that small extra push that overtaxed my heart? Can I even feel the needs of my body over the voice of that insatiable track-and-field coach in my head?

Tshe dato, tshe chima. Do I deserve this heart attack for inventing a meaningless competition with a wonderful woman who isn't even aware of it and only wants to help me through this, who only wants to be my friend? Is it the price of vanity, my inexplicably intense thrill to hear that the cooks are all talking about my stamina and strength?

Frank keeps telling bad, slightly misogynistic jokes to try to get me to stop crying and I want to punch him in the mouth, but I'm probably just mad at him because he had the sense to move more slowly than I. I start to wonder what I've done karmically to deserve dying in the presence of Frank.

I look around again at the glaciers carving valleys into the mountains around me, at the handwoven headdresses and saddle blankets of the yaks, at Karma's sweet and thoughtful countenance, many lifetimes older than his twenty-four years, and I wonder why I have been so deaf to the lessons this landscape has tried to teach me. *Slow down*, it says, everywhere I look. The first lesson of the Buddhist faith: how it's not always about *doing*, but *being*.

What I'd like most of all now is to just *be* for a while, to sit in this meadow until my heart stops beating so fast and my fear seeps away, but there is the fact of three hundred more feet of vertical above me, and five others waiting, and the clock some nonenlightened human being invented ticking, and so I must *do*. I must get myself up and go on, because if something is wrong with my heart, help is four days in that direction, and I'm not enough of a Buddhist yet to sit still in the face of that.

Day Six (later)
Shodu
13,025 feet

So there we were at lunch, Beth being kind and supportive, the cooks force-feeding me soup, me just trying to stop crying long enough to describe how much of the pain remained, thinking about the last couple hundred feet up, thinking the words *I'm scared*, so loud and so incessantly that they're obliterating nearly every other thought in my brain.

I have by then described the pain to Sanjay in such a way that he is scared too, so he is saying how slow we are going to go, how he will walk right in front of me, and Karma will carry my pack and walk right behind, and that's the first hard thing I agree to, but *Okay*, I say, *Karma can carry my pack*.

Then, all of a sudden, for the first time in days, we see a small group of strangers coming up the trail below us: three monks on horseback, two riding, one leading his horse. Karma jumps up, runs down the mountain, and pleads with them to give me a ride on one of the horses up to the top of the pass. They are shouting in Bhutanese across a small canyon;

they argue back and forth, nod their heads, shake their heads, and finally the first monk agrees.

Every part of me wants to turn down the offer, say *No, really I'll be fine*. Every part of me except the part that can't stop crying. I turn to Beth and say, "If I allow this to happen it is a sure sign that I am starting to value my life."

She says, "Just get on the horse, Pam," so I close my eyes for a second and surrender to the outlandish idea of allowing myself to be helped.

Then I walk—slowly—down to those three tiny horses and swing myself up into the saddle of the first one and put my feet into the stirrups, which are hanging no more than six inches down off the saddle's sides. I look like Willie Shoe-maker with my knees up around my ears and my bright Gore-Tex, like a red-and-yellow Humpty Dumpty perched on the skinny spine of that way-too-short horse.

The first monk pulls on the reins and the horse gives a look over his shoulder that says *You've got to be kidding*, and I almost jump off then and say one more time that I'm sure I can walk, but the horse finally starts to move and I let him carry me.

We get halfway up that last three-hundred-foot pitch before the trail gets too rocky and everybody has to dismount. The monk asks for one hundred ngultrums (about three dollars) as payment, and I give him that and a pair of Patagonia gloves (I remember to do it with both hands), and I think they please him a lot.

I walk the rest of the way up with Karma and we say *Lha jaalo* when we get to the top, and I add the prayer flags I bought in Thimpu to the dozens of others and thank Buddha or whoever it is I'm talking to these days for getting me there safely.

Beth and Doug get there next and then Sanjay, who does a headstand and tears off part of his neckerchief to leave as a flag.

When Frank gets there he takes me aside and says, "It must be awful, spending all this money, coming all this way, and then feeling like you cheated right in the final hour."

Beth sticks her tongue out at him and I try real hard not to believe him, but it's what I was thinking every second I was on that horse's back, and now I think, *Where do they come from, all of these lies?* I look around at the mountains, at Karma and all he's tried to teach me, and wonder what it will take—if not this—for me to learn anything at all.

Then we walk down what seems like the longest glaciated valley in the world and watch the horse-riding monks stop from time to time to pick medicinal flowers in front of us. The crazy yaks trot by with all the folding chairs strapped to them, and the snowfields on the peaks above us look like God's own down comforters floating above our heads.

The whole walk down I find myself apologizing over and over to both Karma and Sanjay, telling them about my jockish friend who had aortic separation right out of the blue last year and my mother getting a pain just like that and dying in her sleep that night before she could even contemplate going to the doctor. I wonder aloud if high altitude makes you cry more easily, and joke off the tears as if they'd been an accident, and really begin to hate myself a little more with each apology.

I think of Gautama, how the sight of death made him want

enlightenment, and how he reached down and touched the earth when he finally got it. If there was ever a piece of earth worthy of bearing witness to somebody's enlightenment it was that spot of earth at the top of the Yele La, but I don't know yet if I am a worthy recipient, if I have come away from that experience with a greater understanding of anything.

Karma is patient with me and a little confused. "But Pam," he says, in his quietest, most careful voice, "is it not true that if you *were* having a heart attack it would have been better to be calm about it, to sit quietly and not work yourself up like you did?" I wonder again if a westerner can ever really be a Buddhist, and I reach down and pick up a rock off the tundra and instead of apologizing I say, "I would have, if I could."

Now I'm in my tent, and there is only a hint of pain in my chest and my cough has gotten deeper and harsher—which could, I suppose, have been the source of the pain. Sanjay has been carrying shitake mushrooms and marinara sauce from home so we could have real food for a change, and I know he was saving it for tomorrow—our last night on the trail—but now we are going to have it tonight in honor of the fact that I didn't die.

Beth came by the tent to check on me and she said what happened to me was probably just a wake-up call, and I said I didn't need one, and she said maybe I just thought I didn't, and I think maybe she's right.

Sanjay says I should get an EKG when I get home, so I guess I'll put that on the list with the throat culture and the TB test. The good news is that we are only going down from here (even though the itinerary says there is a great deal of up and down). We won't be above thirteen thousand feet again after tonight—and no matter what, we'll lose five thousand vertical feet in the next two days.

I'm scared, of course, of dying in my sleep tonight like my mother did, but I'm buoyed up slightly by the knowledge that for the first time in my life the people I love won't be disappointed in me for getting a horse ride for approximately 150 feet of a 15,800-foot pass. My first real enlightenment test, I realize, is not to be disappointed in myself.

It's freezing outside. It's freezing in my tent. I'd sell my soul for a Caesar salad and a bowl of hot New England clam chowder. I'd be doing a lot better if I could keep food in my system for more than an hour. Perhaps the spaghetti.

Day Seven
Barshong
12,100 feet

Today was wonderfully uneventful. A long walk up and down, up and down, a spectacular steep canyon full of fall colors, whole mountainsides covered with rhododendron bushes, their leaves every color from deep green to fluorescent red. A long lunch on a hot rock in the sunshine and early to camp. We're having a slumber party tonight in a smoky little trail house.

Tonight the yak herders, the kitchen staff, and Karma will perform for us a series of Bhutanese folk songs and dances, steps and lyrics that Karma assures me every single person in Bhutan knows. We will be asked to reciprocate, and when we cast about for something that all six of us Americans know, all we can come up with is the national anthem, "If I Had a Hammer," and the Hokey Pokey (which the yak herders already know, having been taught it by groups of American tourists who have come before). Beth and I think that under pressure we can do all twenty-four verses of "American Pie."

Across the meadow Karma is practicing throwing a lasso like an American cowboy, and I just got a quick lesson from the yak herders on how to throw it the Bhutanese way.

I'm quite happy to report that today I wasn't the first in camp.

Day Eight
Thimpu trailhead
7,900 feet (According to Frank's watch, we've done a total of 26,000 vertical feet altogether, up and down, up and down, over the last eight days.)

Our itinerary for today began with the words THIS IS NOT AN EASY DAY, and it wasn't. Twenty miles of mud-slogging, a lot of it right behind the yak herders, listening to them coo and shout to the yaks, watching them throw rocks at their butts to keep them moving, the yaks sinking into the mud sometimes to their bellies, making the trail even tougher for us.

At one point I pushed Karma into the mud accidentally and then I fell in even deeper and I said, "Now that's instant Karma for you," the first time I'd dared to make a joke on his name.

When at last we got down to the level of the Thimpu River and I asked Karma how far it was to the end of the trail, he said, "We will walk along the river for some time," and it was the first time I didn't find the Bhutanese way of measuring hours all that charming.

"How much time?" I said, but he only smiled at me

sweetly, and I thought of something he'd said days ago, that enlightenment is a firefly, not a flashlight, and I took a deep breath and vowed to enjoy every step of the trek that remained, no matter how damn many there were.

I'm in the outfitting company tent now, surrounded by doughnuts and sandwiches and bottles of beer. The bus is running, and if Frank ever shows up we'll head for the hotel. Doug suggests that the yak herders go back up the trail and throw rocks at Frank's butt to get him moving, an idea that gets everyone's approval, but nobody moves. The owner of the Bhutanese outfitter is there with a present for us, silk scarves imprinted with the eight lucky signs in honor of completing our journey, and elation and exhaustion are fighting for purchase inside me.

It's early in the morning on my last full day in Bhutan, and I'm going through the familiar melancholy of leaving a place I have fallen in love with. I am an expert at this emotion, and my career choice affords me the opportunity to experience it several times a year. But it is possible that this leaving will be the hardest ever, because of the things the country and Karma have tried to teach me, and because of all the places I have been in the world, I think I love the land of the friendly dragon most of all.

I'll miss all the village children who still haven't cried, and who today, as if they can feel my imminent departure, scribble their addresses for me on a pad. I'll miss the rice fields and the hand-painted houses that sit beside them, the fields of purple cosmos and the monks who walk their edges in robes of bright orange and yellow under the orange-yellow sun. I'll miss the *dzongs* and their hidden prayer rooms, the terrible roads and the excellent drivers, the chilies and cheese, the red rice, the pine trees, the endless river gorges, and Jhomolhari, stoic, watching over it all. I'll miss the way the Bhutanese shake their heads in a gesture so much like *no* that means *yes*, the thick throaty sound of the Dzonka language, the *some time* of everything here, the tremendous compassion that is, every moment, a part of these people's lives.

I'll miss Beth too, her quiet presence and confident gait, but I know we'll see each other again, in New York or Colorado. Perhaps one day we'll even embark on another trip. More than anyone I'll miss Karma, his shy smile, soft hands, and elegant pride, his genuine willingness to be in every moment, a presence that lends grace to a clumsy world.

At the same time I'm eager, as always, to move forward. I want to go home and put my arms—Bhutanese-style—around everyone I love. I want to start an American Folk Singing and Dancing Club. I want to paint my bedroom in thick stripes of red, green, and blue.

My mind is already dancing around the words *Mongolia* and *Antarctica*, proving I'm not cured of my wanderlust and may never be. The better part of me hopes that on those trips I'll slow down even further. I have promised myself that on my next trek I will make every effort not to notice what order people arrive in camp. I know that enlightenment isn't a flashlight, it's a firefly, or in the case of Bhutan, a whole field of them, illuminating my landscape on both the inside and the outside, showing me just as much truth as I am ready to see.

HOME IS
where
YOUR DOGS
ARE

———

Home Is Where
Your Dogs Are

M y dog Jackson died today. He was my first dog, and I bought him at a pet store when he was only eight weeks old. We've been together more than fourteen years, which makes our relationship the longest successful relationship of my life. By far. There have been many times during those years when I thought if he were to die, I wouldn't be able to live without him.

Fourteen is old for a dog of Jackson's size (just over a hundred pounds) and these last few years he hasn't been doing very well. He went deaf first, probably the result of listening to the sound of his own bark for so many years, then blind, then crippled with arthritis. He became increasingly disoriented. If he barked at the door to go out and I opened it, he would walk around behind the open door so that he could go through the dog door that was cut into its base. Sometimes he got stuck staring into a corner, and had to bark until somebody came over and helped him get turned around.

The people who've met Jackson these last few years can't even imagine the dog he once was. How he ran the length of countless beaches and swam in three of the world's seven oceans, how he hiked in fifty-seven of our country's wilderness areas and national parks. They wouldn't have been able to imagine how, when we got to places along the trail where the Park Service had installed ladders to help a hiker get over a particularly difficult piece of rock, Jackson would allow me to place all four of his paws on the rungs of the ladder. They wouldn't have been able to imagine how he could keep up with my pickup truck going thirty-five miles an hour for a distance of over a mile.

For most of his life, Jackson took every risk, met every challenge, climbed every mountain, and forded every stream he found in front of him. He rode in the truck bed with one paw on the wheel well and one paw dangling over the highway. He sat at scenic overlooks—always—with two paws over the edge of the cliff.

My safety, of course, was a much different matter, and he took his role as protector very seriously. Swimming with him was almost impossible because he was constantly trying to rescue me, his paws flailing around my head and my shoulders, his claws splayed and scratching my skin. After we moved to the ranch he was always trying to protect me from the horses. He would spend his whole morning sitting out in the pasture and barking at them, and then he'd come in, as if punching out on the clock for a food-and-water break, do a quick check-in with me, and head back out.

When we lived in Park City, Jackson brought home to me any number of wonderful presents: a five-gallon container of rainbow sherbet, a freshly cleaned deer head, a twenty-six-pound turkey that someone had left on the back stoop to thaw.

In Oakland he kept me company when there was no one else to do that, and his allergic reaction to the fleas there was one of the reasons we all came to our senses and came back home.

Home. That word again. And it occurs to me today that for many years home was, above all else, with Jackson and our red Mazda truck. That truck still runs, eleven years and 225,000 miles later, though I only use it now for garbage, river trips, and hay. He loved that truck almost as much as he loved me, and he was always happy when we were in it going somewhere. I had only to walk out the front door of wherever we were living, and he was up and into the truck bed, hoping that if he looked enthusiastic enough I might drop whatever I was doing and decide to go on a trip.

Sometimes it worked, because a trip to anywhere usually sounded better than where we were. I was running away from myself in those days, and Jackson, well, he was always just running. Home was a place we rented, a place to sleep, and if it was clean enough, to cook dinner every now and then. Largely it was a place where we could spread the maps out and plan the next trip.

Jackson and I lived in some first-class dumps back in those days, though none of them dumpier than a sheepherder's trailer called the *African Queen* in Fraser, Colorado, that rented for seventy-five dollars a month and had no running water and a little Army cookstove that only burned for two hours at a time. The *Queen* sat on land that was part of a commune run by a beautiful eighty-year-old born-again hippie lady named Grandma Miller who walked two miles each day in the Colorado mountains and made us sing around the campfire "Will the Circle Be Unbroken" every night before bed.

Fraser, Colorado, was known as *the icebox of the nation*, the coldest place most often recorded in the continental United States, until the nearby ski area people decided that the icebox reputation was bad for business and had the weather station moved to Granby, fifteen miles upriver and balmy by comparison.

In the years Jackson and I lived in the *Queen*, I would come home from my job as a restaurant dishwasher on one sixty-below-zero night after another with all the steak scraps I could carry. I'd pack my little stove with wood, and cover my body with, in this order, my flannel union suit, flannel nightgown, wool hat, wool gloves, wool socks, wool scarf, and down booties. I'd feed Jackson all twenty pounds of steak fat, get under my three or four down sleeping bags, and Jackson would get on top of the pile and metabolize all night.

The ranch I live on now, the ranch that I (with a little help from the Bank of Creede, Colorado) actually own, is a far cry from the *African Queen*. Though not exactly luxurious, my two-bedroom ranch house is overbuilt to withstand the long winters, the frequent seventy-mile-an-hour winds, and the nine-thousand-feet ultraviolet rays that turn a paint job to dust in a few short summers. I have plenty of running well water—inside. I have a woodstove that will burn for twelve hours and propane heat that will run for months by itself.

But it is the land that the house sits on that matters: 120 acres in the center of a high mountain meadow tucked up and under the sharp-edged backbone of the Continental Divide. The Divide winds over 25,000 miles through two continents, from northern Alaska to Tierra del Fuego, separating the drainages of two oceans at all times, and we live in the shadow of a curve so deep that it surrounds our valley on more than three sides. The Rio Grande, as clear and dazzling as a river can be, follows the curve of the mountains past my ranch only minutes from where it is born on the highest eastern slope of the high San Juans. The fields are covered with lupine, paintbrush, and wild irises, except in winter, when they are covered with snow that stays white the whole winter long. I have a barn right out of Big Valley, that smells like old hay and pack rats, that sits in the afternoon shadow of the mountain. Given all the trailers and basement apartments and rent-a-buses we've lived in, I am not surprised that Jackson kept his eye on the driveway, waiting for the real owners to come home and send us down the road in our bright red Mazda truck.

Jackson couldn't get into the truck by himself these last years. Some of my friends said I should put him down, but I have always let him make his own decisions, and it didn't seem right to change the rules on him this late in the game. Last year when he became incontinent, *he* decided he didn't want to come in the house anymore, even when I urged him to on the coldest nights.

"You wouldn't put your grandmother to sleep just because she had to wear diapers" is what I said to my friends, but in my own mind I had another measure of Jackson's quality of life. If he ever stopped being mad at the horses, if he ever stopped hobbling out there at least once a day and giving them an earful for no apparent reason, then it would be time to consider euthanasia. He was out there barking at the horses the morning he disappeared.

I began this essay by saying, "Jackson died today," but I should have said, "Today is the day I gave up thinking he might still hobble home." Actually, Jackson disappeared, as if into thin air, and although three humans and three dogs have walked every square inch of this ranch and its surroundings, we can't find hide nor hair of him. Which is strange, because given his physical condition, he couldn't have gone far.

It's likely that if he walked off somewhere to die, the coyotes would have taken his body. It is also possible, if he got too far away from the house, that the coyotes would have taken him alive.

In his last months, Jackson had embarked on a series of what my ex-husband, Mike, would call *walkabouts*. Sometimes a day—or even a day and a night—would go by and I wouldn't have any idea where he was. Then the next morning he'd be sleeping on the porch as usual. I saw these walkabouts as a sign that his time was near.

Maybe he was trying to let me gradually get used to his absence. Maybe he had pain he couldn't tell me about, and was asking the coyotes to come. Maybe he knew I wouldn't be able to stand seeing his body, so every time he thought it might be the end he went out for the night and waited. The non-dog-person explanation, of course, is that he got increasingly disoriented and finally lost—which is possible, but I doubt it, and I'm the one who lived with him for more than fourteen years.

I can't decide whether or not I want him to have been alive when the coyotes took him. I know that sounds terrible, but he did so always love a good scrap. I'd like to believe a pagan god visited the ranch, stole his body just before the moment of death, and threw him into the sky to become a new constellation, but the coyote scenario seems more likely. It's a death he would have written for himself, a death that does justice to his life.

Dante, the wolfhound, is lying on the floor as usual, raising his eyebrows at me as I write this. *Jackson who?* is the question behind those eyebrows—my two male dogs had developed quite the rivalry in the last two years. Even if Dante could speak he might not dare to tell me the rest of what he's thinking: *As soon as you get over this, you'll have much more time for me.*

When it's Dante's time to leave the earth, death-by-coyote will not be his chosen method. He'd like to find himself in a private room in one of the country's best vet hospitals, the air thick with flowers, all his dog and human friends gathered lovingly around.

Last Thanksgiving, David and I took Dante camping in Utah's newly sanctioned Escalante–Golden Staircase National Monument. It was our first time there, and Dante's first real road trip. There were rivers to swim in, rocks to climb around, lizards to chase, rib-eye steaks on the grill to share, and our constant attention—the perfect formula to make any dog jump for joy. And Dante did swim in the river, climb the rocks, chase the lizards, eat the rib-eye, but he did all of it without much enthusiasm, as though his purpose was mostly to humor us. In the moments between all the fun he would lay his long body down, put his head on his paws, and sigh, *This is nice and all, but when do we get to go home?*

We took a long walk that weekend down Deer Creek Canyon, where the cottonwoods were still holding on to the last of their leaves and the mule deer were thick and fat, storing up what they could for the winter. The sky, which had looked threatening all weekend, finally opened into a downpour, and we ran for the shelter of an abandoned line camp, a two-room rat-infested tin shed, surrounded by beer cans and whiskey bottles. Two beat-up chairs sat inside the doorway, and we scraped the rat shit off their seats and sat down. Dante made nervous circles around the tiny room, and finally lay down and let out a huge mournful sigh.

"This is our new home," I told him. "How do you like it?" His eyebrows twitched from my face to David's and back to mine.

"Look around," David said. "Go pick out your bedroom."

Dante thumped his tail meekly and let out another soft groan.

When the rain slowed and I went to see if we might brave it, he was out the door and down the trail so fast there was nothing to do but follow. He didn't really perk up again until he recognized the last turn for the ranch.

Hard as it is for me to imagine, Dante turns out to be a dog who would just as soon not travel, and Sally, his Aussie/coyote sidekick, is even worse. There's an ever-expanding part of me that can't blame them. When you live in doggie paradise, why would you ever want to leave?

And we do live in paradise, the mountains that form the Divide holding my ranch as though it has cupped us in the palm of its hand, or like a horseshoe laid on its side and turned up at the ends to keep all the luck from spilling out. We feel safe here, protected by this natural fortress of rock face and scree field the way someone else might take comfort in a stone fence or brick wall.

Safety is important to Dante, and as I've said again and again—as if constantly trying to convince myself—it's also important to me. The metaphorical significance of today's changing of the guard dog is far from lost on me. Among Jackson's regrets in his final hour was likely that he never made it to that fourth ocean. My number-one dog, as of this minute, is a dog who loves more than anything else to stay home.

It took me a long time to call this ranch mine. I'd always get stuck on the words *I own*, or *my ranch*. Part of it, I know, was a leftover from my days with Grandma Miller and the gang in the *African Queen* when we were all dishwashers and bus drivers and we thought that owning a 120-acre ranch would qualify us as first-class criminals. We thought we'd never own anything, we were all so wild and free.

Freedom's just another word for nothing left to lose, Janis sang, and I still haven't forgotten. For the first time in my life, the what-I've-got-to-lose column is practically overflowing, and though the ranch is only one item on that list, it is not separate from the others. This is such a magical place, so supremely calm, strong, and honest, that it is hard for me to believe I deserve it. I am constantly trying to earn my right to be here, to live up to the person (calm, strong, and honest) this place constantly asks me to be. The commitment this place necessitates is turning me into a person who is capable of commitment, to all kinds of things I never imagined, and I understand, now, the main reason I was afraid to call this place mine.

Like any other thing—a friend, a man, a dog—I was afraid that if I loved the ranch I might lose it. I might not be able to make a payment, or it might burn down in a summer lightning storm, or maybe I'd sell it one day in a gesture (and God knows I've made them before) from the center of my own fear and stupidity. But the ranch has also shown me I now have a measure of control over my own decisions. I'm not so afraid of making those kinds of mistakes anymore.

A hundred and twenty acres isn't much by Colorado standards, but it's mine to care for, that ponderosa pine tree, that fence line, my pack rat hotel of a barn. I am attached to it, responsible for it, grateful for the attachment, grateful for the beauty that I fall into every single day. And when I pull in the driveway and stare down the mountains along the Divide, when I wake up to the sunshine on three new feet of snow, when the alpenglow is lighting only the very tip of Red Mountain above me, I know that this is the first real home I've ever had, and I'll do whatever is required to keep it.

Home is where your dogs are, I've said many times, but now it means something entirely different. Now it means a ranch in Colorado, *my* ranch in Colorado, the first place from which I don't feel the need to run away. Now it means just three dogs, and a fourth one I'll always love whose bones are scattered somewhere out across the pasture. I no longer feel like I won't be able to live without him. He saw me through the loneliest years, the transient years, the years I couldn't attach myself to anyplace or anything, years that I needed to live through, before I could find my way home.

There will be more dogs laid to rest here, and horses, and maybe one day, even me. In the meantime, I'm going to go outside and take my remaining three dogs walking. We'll go up to the top of the hill and howl a little elegy for Jackson. Tonight we'll look for the shape of his bones in the sky.